THE COMPLETE GUIDE TO TIBETAN TERRIERS

Roxanne James

Publication Data

Roxanne James
The Complete Guide to Tibetan Terriers – First edition.
Summary: "Successfully raising a Tibetan Terrier dog from puppy to old age"
– Provided by publisher.
ISBN: 978-1-954288-37-9
[1. Tibetan Terrier – Non-Fiction] I. Title.

Design by Sorin Rădulescu
First paperback edition, 2021

TABLE OF CONTENTS

CHAPTER 1
Tibetan Terriers: History and Characteristics

Holy Dog of Tibet

The Tibetan Terrier (TT) is an ancient breed of dog originating from the spiritual center of Buddhism, high in the mountains of Tibet in Asia. The breed was created by Buddhist monks, also known as lamas, which is how they earned the name 'Holy Dog.' Monks prized the Tibetan Terrier as watchdogs and close companions. However, the canines also played an active role beyond the monasteries where they were born.

In ancient times, the Tibetan Terrier was considered to be extremely lucky. Nomadic herdsmen would take the dogs with them on their travels across the high plateaus and have them stand guard over their tents by night. Neither the lamas nor the herdsmen would ever sell their Tibetan Terriers, preferring to give them as gifts to esteemed officials or in return for favors or services.

HELPFUL TIP

Tibetan Terrier Club of America (TTCA)

The Tibetan Terrier Club of America (TTCA) is the official American Kennel Club (AKC) parent club for Tibetan Terriers. The TTCA encourages breeders to accept the AKC breed standard for Tibetan Terriers and aims to preserve the breed's interests. The group also hosts obedience trials and specialty shows throughout the year. Members of the TTCA receive the TT Times, the club's bi-monthly newsletter, and may be entitled to club voting rights depending on their membership category. For more information, visit www.ttca-online.org.

Origins and Emergence of Tibetan Terriers

The Tibetan Terrier emerged from its remote location when one was gifted to Dr. Agnes RH Greig. A Tibetan man was so grateful to Dr. Greig for saving his wife's life that he gave her a prized TT pup in thanks. The doctor named the female puppy Bunti, and after acquiring a male, she established a breeding program in India. This launched the breed to a much wider world, and it was given the name Tibetan Terrier, even though the dog merely resembles one in terms of size. The breed standard was created in India by its Kennel Club in 1930, going on to achieve recognition by England's Kennel Club seven years later.

It was almost two decades later that the Tibetan Terrier arrived in the United States in 1956. The dog, named Gremlin Cortina, was owned by Dr. Henry and Alice Murphy, who were so enamored with their companion that they established their own breeding kennels. In 1957, the Tibetan Terrier Club of America was formed, and in 1973, the breed finally achieved full recognition by the American Kennel Club.

Photo Courtesy of Karen Dean

Photo Courtesy of Daniel and Kay Rayner

Appearance and Variations

The Tibetan Terrier bears more than a passing resemblance to the Lhasa Apso, the breed's smaller cousin. At the smaller end of medium-sized breeds, the TT stands at around 15 inches from the shoulder and weighs between 20 and 24 pounds. One of the hallmarks of the breed is its amazing layered coat; a long and fine topcoat disguises two thick, wooly layers underneath, which provides the Tibetan Terrier with highly effective insulation.

Tibetan Terriers have a variety of colors, including white, gold, silver, black, brindle, and tricolor, although they may have a combination of other colors too. They have deep, dark eyes that are large and wide-set, pendant ears, a black nose, and a feathery tail. TTs have strong muzzles and teeth with a scissor or reverse scissor bite. Their jaws are powerful, and they often sport a small beard.

One feature that is completely unique to the Tibetan Terrier is the feet. Designed to act as snowshoes in the harsh Tibetan terrain, they are large and round with no arch so that they are completely flat to the ground. There is thick hair between the TT's toes and pads, which acts as both insulation and protection when walking in the snow-covered mountains.

Overview of Temperament and Characteristics

The most important aspects of Tibetan Terriers you need to consider before getting one are personality and temperament. You need to know what's going on beneath that irresistibly cute exterior and decide whether these characteristics suit your own personality and lifestyle.

Generally speaking, the Tibetan Terrier is ultra-intelligent, extremely cheeky, and has an almost cat-like attitude of "what's in it for me?" This can make them stubborn. This is a breed that requires early training and behavioral management to prevent the dogs from developing bad habits.

Something that you should bear in mind when considering taking on a Tibetan Terrier is their need to be in your company as much as possible. These are dogs that don't handle isolation very well at all, which is almost certainly a nod to their origins as monks' companions and guardians. In return for this slight neediness, your Tibetan Terrier will shower you with an abundance of loyalty, love, and devotion.

Although Tibetan Terriers look more like Disney dogs than fearsome warriors, they have an extremely strong instinct to guard their territory, which is your home and everyone in it! This makes it essential to be proactive in your dog's training from the start by giving him clear, consistent, calm directions. Tibetan Terriers have a strong desire to please, and rewards work very well with this breed, even if they're not edible!

Another instinct that can make Tibetan Terriers difficult to train is the breed's herding instinct, developed from their time spent with the nomadic herdsmen. For today's Tibetan Terriers, this herding instinct can make them very unreliable off a leash as they are easily distracted by other people and dogs.

Photo Courtesy
of Cody and Jillian Taplin

Health and Fitness of Your Tibetan Terrier

> *Tibetans are athletic, so if you want to hike for 10 miles they will hike with you for 10 miles. However, if on the other hand, you want to sleep for 10 hours they are the first ones to look at you and say 'oh, its time to get up already?' They are a very versatile breed in that sense.*
>
> NIKKIE KINZIGER
> *Ri Lee Kennels*

Tibetan Terriers have an average lifespan of 12-15 years and are prone to some major health problems with their eyes, such as progressive retinal atrophy (PRA) and lens luxation. The breed also has a disposition for minor skeletal problems like patellar luxation and canine hip dysplasia (CHD).

Degenerative conditions such as cataracts and ceroid lipofuscinosis are common in Tibetan Terriers, along with hypothyroidism, a condition that can be successfully treated with a specifically prescribed diet.

In terms of exercise, Tibetan Terriers require daily walks of around 30 minutes minimum, which you can split into a couple of walks or one longer one depending on what best suits your routine.

It's probably not surprising that Tibetan Terriers have the capacity to walk for several hours, as their ancestors travailed with herdsmen in the rugged terrain of the Trans Himalayas. Although TTs are small, they are extremely robust, and their long, thick coats protect them from the coldest of temperatures.

TTs absolutely adore hiking, swimming, or running with their humans, and they have the energy to keep up. Nevertheless, don't be surprised if they give you the puppy eyes routine to ask to be scooped up into your arms. They may not necessarily be tired, but from time to time, they'll want to enjoy the view from your level.

Tibetan Terriers are extremely bright, and consequently, they like to be stimulated, even when on a routine walk. Having plenty of off-leash time to allow them to explore their surroundings makes walks fun for TTs because of their inexhaustible curiosity.

That said, if you're not able to dedicate many walking hours to your TT through the working week, they will adapt to that very quickly. Just so long as you take at least half an hour out of your daily routine for a refreshing constitutional with your TT, they'll be happy and healthy.

TTs are also very adaptable to the kind of property you live in. Being relatively small and compact, Tibetan Terriers don't need a huge amount of space. Whether you're in an apartment with no outside space or a ranch with acres of land to wander, your TT will only ever want to be where you are.

Photo Courtesy
of Hannah Howard

Is a Tibetan Terrier the Right Fit for You?

Tibetan Terriers can adapt to homes which are urban, suburban or farm. They are happy with children and other animals, but they are most happy in a home in which they get to spend lots of time with their human companions.

JACKIE FAUST
Arkeden Tibetan Terriers

In order to help with your decision, it's a good idea to consider the pros and cons of a Tibetan Terrier. In summary:

PROS

- Affectionate and dependable
- Highly intelligent and responsive to training
- Beautiful appearance with a coat that doesn't shed
- Sociable with other pets and children of all ages

CONS

- Known for excessive barking
- Despite no shedding, a high maintenance coat
- High energy levels, requiring plenty of exercise
- Propensity for stubbornness
- Prone to separation anxiety

CHAPTER 2
Choosing Your Tibetan Terrier Puppy

Should You Get a Puppy or Adult Tibetan Terrier?

When considering bringing a Tibetan Terrier into your life, most people imagine a picture-perfect puppy that's irresistibly cute. Not only are you getting the best cuddle partner when you have a puppy TT, but you also get the chance to parent and shape them to be your own. However, with all that cuddly cuteness comes a few challenges, so don't be deceived by those puppy eyes!

Puppy TTs are extremely hard work, easily as time-consuming and challenging as a toddler. They require more time, patience, and often more money than an adult Tibetan Terrier. If you're not able to be at home for most of the day, a TT pup might not be the best fit for you. TT pups also need to be spayed or neutered and require various vaccinations and more attention from the vet than most middle-aged dogs.

There's more to take into account if you're considering homing an adult Tibetan Terrier. Here's a list of the pros and cons:

FUN FACT
A Symbol of Luck

Tibetan Terriers originated in Buddhist monasteries, where they were bred as watchdogs and companion animals. These dogs were treasured as holy dogs and were often given as gifts intended to bestow good luck upon the receiver. Because Tibetan Terriers were considered emblems of good luck, it was viewed as bad luck to mistreat them in any way.

PROS

- Most adult Tibetan Terriers in shelters or for sale privately are house-trained. They are more likely to have had some basic command training, too, such as sit, stay, and come.

- If a Tibetan Terrier is coming from a shelter or foster parent, they will have evaluated the dog's personality and behavior. They will be able to tell you if a TT is good with kids and other animals too.

- Adult TTs are typically much lower maintenance than puppies, mostly because they tend to get in much less trouble! An adult TT is less likely to be as needy of your attention as a pup, making them generally easier to parent.

- Although owning a dog is not cheap, vets' fees are generally at the lowest when they are young adults through to middle-age. You'll save money with an adult TT as they will probably have been spayed/neutered and microchipped too.

CONS

- An adult Tibetan Terrier is just as cute as a puppy, although it is a completely different dog-owning experience. Some people want to share every moment of their TT's lives.

- Adult dogs may have developed bad habits which can be difficult to un-train. If this is the case, it is always best to find a canine behavioral trainer to help you.

- When you get an adult Tibetan Terrier, you won't know its history. You should be able to get an idea of how past experiences have affected the dog from the shelter or foster parent. You should understand that there could be things or environments that frighten your TT that you won't be able to predict.

Buying from a Breeder vs. Adoption

One of the biggest decisions you will make when choosing your Tibetan Terrier pup is whether to adopt or purchase from a breeder. Please avoid pet stores and do not support them by buying your Tibetan Terrier from them. Pet stores are known to keep their puppies in unsatisfactory conditions, and they acquire them directly from puppy mills, where Tibetan Terriers are inhumanely bred for profit.

As with every major decision, it's always a good idea to layout the pros and cons of both your options, in this case, adoption versus buying from a breeder.

Adopting or Rescuing a Tibetan Terrier

All dog lovers want to rescue canines that have been abandoned and abused. Despite this, many people think that shelter dogs come with behavioral issues or bad habits that will make them unpredictable, particularly in a family setting. This is simply not true because dogs are not always surrendered to shelters because of behavioral problems.

Changes in family situations or the death of an owner are often reasons for dogs to be given up. In these cases, it is very likely that your Tibetan Terrier has already had some training or experience living with children and other pets in the past. This can actually be a very good reason to consider adoption, particularly if you're looking for an adult Tibetan Terrier.

Photo Courtesy of Mr and Mrs C. Davies

BENEFITS

- When you rescue a dog, you create space for another to take its place at the shelter, which means you are actually saving two dogs.
- Many Tibetan Terriers in shelters will have had their necessary vaccinations and may also have been spayed/neutered and microchipped.
- Shelters get to know their Tibetan Terrier charges well so that they can place them with the most suitable homes. You'll find out a lot about your TT's personality from the staff so that there won't be any surprises when you bring him home.
- Adult Tibetan Terriers will have been housetrained, which will save you a lot of time in training.
- A private rescue shelter will take your Tibetan Terrier back if you find that he isn't a good fit for you.
- The love your Tibetan Terrier will heap on you for bringing him into your life will be unlike anything you've ever experienced from an animal.

CHALLENGES

- When you adopt a Tibetan Terrier from a shelter, you might not know how he will behave in your home environment. The shelter staff can give you helpful tips, but just bear in mind that the adjustment could take time.
- Tibetan Terriers have a tendency for separation anxiety because they enjoy human company so much. Your shelter dog may have been traumatized by his past experience, which may exacerbate the panic caused by separation. You ideally need to be in a position to spend as much time with your new companion as possible, taking time off from work if necessary until he adjusts to your routine.
- There are some health conditions that Tibetan Terriers are prone to, such as hip dysplasia, autoimmune thyroiditis, and problems with their eyes. If you are rescuing or adopting your Tibetan Terrier, make sure you get as much of his medical history from the shelter as you can. If there are any doubts about a TT's behavior, he is best off being adopted by an experienced dog owner.

Buying Your Tibetan Terrier from a Breeder

> *If possible, make a visit to the breeder's home or at the very least, get a recommendation from a friend who may know of the breeder and their reputation. If neither of those is possible, when you do speak to a breeder, ask for their references. If you do visit, ask to see the parents or any lineage of the prospective puppy. This will give you a chance to see temperaments and behaviors in their packs.*
>
> NIKKIE KINZIGER
> *Ri Lee Kennels*

If you are thinking about buying your Tibetan Terrier puppy from a breeder, it is vital that you choose the right one. We'll go into more depth about what to look for in a breeder in a while, but in the meantime, let's take a look at the benefits and challenges of purchasing a Tibetan Terrier from a breeder.

BENEFITS

- You will be able to meet your Tibetan Terrier pup's mother and check out the environment the puppy has been raised in.
- The most reputable breeders will provide you with the results of genetic testing to show your dog has not inherited any genetic health conditions.
- You'll be able to train your Tibetan Terrier from the earliest point in his life.
- You'll know exactly what you're getting in terms of the Tibetan Terrier's characteristics, and you can also gain very helpful knowledge and understanding from the breeder.

CHALLENGES

- There are plenty of Tibetan Terriers dying in dog shelters every year, and buying from a breeder doesn't give you the option to save one of them.
- No matter how small and harmless they look, a Tibetan Terrier is HARD WORK in the early days and is a similar commitment to a human baby! It's easy to get caught up in a TT's charm and forget about the hours of your time he will demand.

14

- You have to focus on training from day one as an untrained Tibetan Terrier will present you with endless challenges further down the line.
- Buying a Tibetan Terrier pup from a breeder can be very expensive, and you will also have to factor vet bills into the equation.

Photo Courtesy of Lorna Hook

Tips for Locating a Reputable Breeder

Finding the right breeder is imperative to ensure you have a happy and healthy Tibetan Terrier. Here are some tips to help you:

1 The best place to inquire about reputable Tibetan Terrier breeders is the Tibetan Terrier Club of America (TTCA). The TTCA has a Breeder Referral Coordinator (BRC) program, which is designed to connect their members who are breeders with people interested in acquiring a Tibetan Terrier.

2 Regardless of how well-known the breeder is, ask for a written health guarantee or contract. This should include such things as a lifetime return policy, a vet visit within a specific time period, and a spay/neuter agreement. Reputable breeders will have a template agreement precisely for this purpose, and you should ask to see it early in your discussions.

3 Find out as much as you can about your TT pup's parents, grandparents, and siblings. The Orthopedic Foundation for Animals (OFA) has a hip rating for Tibetan Terriers, and a breeder should be able to tell you whether your pup and his parents have been rated fair, good, or excellent. This is important as Tibetan Terriers have a propensity for hip dysplasia.

4 Eyes are a potential problem area for Tibetan Terriers. Ask the breeder if your pup's parents have had their eyes checked by the Canine Eye Registration Foundation (CERF). Request a paper copy of the OFA rating and the CERF eye checks from the breeder.

5 Ask if there is any history of cancer, heart disease, or autoimmune issues in the TT pup's pedigree. Although uncommon, these genetic diseases can be more prevalent in Tibetan Terriers.

6 Ask breeders if they microchip pups before they leave the premises.

7 A reputable breeder will provide you with registration papers from the United Kennel Club or American Kennel Club covering five generations of your pup's pedigree.

8 Obtain an up-to-date record of inoculations together with a certificate of good health from a vet dated within the past 10 to 14 days.

9 Take into account the age of the mother and make sure she is not too young to be breeding (under the age of two).

Photo Courtesy of Alexandra Marckx

10 Ask breeders if they have conducted any evaluations on the litter of pups in terms of structure and temperament.

11 See if the breeder can provide you with feeding suggestions and vaccination timelines for your Tibetan Terrier pup.

12 When you have chosen your Tibetan Terrier and taken him home with you, visit your vet within three days.

Choosing Your Puppy

When you are confronted with a litter of Tibetan Terrier pups, you will no doubt want them all! If choosing the best pup for you were just about appearance, you would be hard pushed to make a choice. However, you have to steel yourself and make a thorough evaluation so that you single out one cute little bundle to call your own.

17

Here are the steps you can take to make your choice a little easier:

- Talk to the breeder or owner about the pups' appetite and eliminations. Are they eating dry puppy food, and if so, what type? Have they had any issues such as vomiting or diarrhea and been checked for intestinal parasites? Bear in mind that all pups should have worming treatments every two weeks from the age of two weeks.

- Observe the littermates interacting with each other. Do they play together, or is there one that seems much quieter than the rest? One TT pup may stand out from the litter and display a dominant personality. You can tell a great deal about TT pups by the way they socialize with their parents and siblings.

- Look at the overall appearance of the TT pups. Are their coats shiny and untangled? Are there any bald spots or skin issues that are noticeable? Healthy TT pups should have coats that are thick but light, with a lustrous sheen. Don't forget that adult TT's coats are profuse and layered over with long, shiny locks, and your puppy's coat has some way to go yet!

- Watch the puppies move to check that they have full mobility. Does one of them have a limp? Although TT puppies are generally quite clumsy when they walk, they should be able to bear weight evenly on all four legs.

When you have observed the littermates interacting, it's time to look at an individual TT that has caught your eye. Pay attention to the following areas:

- **Eyes:** They should be clear and without any redness or discharge. There shouldn't be any hair loss around the eyes, and the pup should not rub at his eyes or squint.

- **Ears:** They should not have any odor or discharge, and the pup's ear-flaps should be covered in healthy hair. If you notice a TT pup scratching at its ears, it may have an ear infection.

- **Nose:** It's ok if there is a little clear discharge from the nose, but if it is discolored, that is not normal. Your TT pup should breathe easily and without any noise from their nose.

- **Head:** If a TT pup has a small soft spot at the top of its head, this could be a sign of possible problems with the bones or plates of the skull.

- **Mouth:** A TT pup's gums should be moist with a healthy pink color. Check how the jaw closes and that the top and bottom teeth align.

- **Belly:** If there is a protrusion around a TT pup's navel, it can indicate an umbilical hernia which sometimes requires surgical correction.

- **Skin:** Check for areas of hair loss, pustules (infected pimples), redness, or flaking.

Ultimately, when choosing a Tibetan Terrier breeder, you have to trust your intuition. You must be able to visit the breeders' premises, so don't rely on purely online communications as a way of choosing. Remember, it's the start of a wonderful journey for both you and your pup, so you want to be careful about laying the best foundations by getting to know him before taking him home.

It's a Family Affair

Finding the right Tibetan Terrier should be a decision that involves every member of the household. Although some may think a surprise gift of a Tibetan Terrier pup may be an amazing idea, it's always unwise to suddenly introduce a pup to a new human—and vice versa!

Getting any dog MUST be a considered decision. Before you even think about getting a dog, you should evaluate your circumstances. Do you live alone and work long hours? Do you regularly have a houseful of teenagers? If you have other pets, are they likely to get along with a new pup?

WHERE you live is as important in the decision process as HOW you live. Do you live in an apartment without easy access to an outside space? Are

19

you in a gated community with neighboring dogs or other animals? Perhaps your home is in a remote location?

In essence, you need to view your life and your home through your pup's eyes, and importantly, every single family member should be involved in sharing responsibility for the dog's care.

When you are visiting a breeder or shelter to find your Tibetan Terrier, take everyone along with you. It's very worthwhile seeing where your new companion came from as it helps you determine what kind of temperament the dog will have. You want to observe litters or individual pups in their present environment for a few visits before choosing a pup to invite into your life.

As a parent, I can vouch for the significant life lessons dogs can teach young children. Although my two kids are now fully grown, they are both dog owners themselves who take their responsibilities very seriously. Of course, the harshest life lesson of all will be a long way off when it comes time to say goodbye to your Tibetan Terrier, but the joy they will leave in your heart will last forever.

Take as much time as you need to find the right Tibetan Terrier for you and everyone he'll share his life with. Just like us, Tibetan Terriers are emotional creatures that thrive on human interaction. They have their up days and down days too. If you think about it, we choose the people we want to be friends with, and so finding the right Tibetan Terrier for you isn't very different at all!

CHAPTER 3

Preparing Your Home for a Tibetan Terrier

Getting Small Children Adjusted

Children can have a fantastic relationship with the family dog, although much depends on how they are introduced to the canine as a puppy. One of your responsibilities as a Tibetan Terrier owner is to ensure all the important relationships get off to a flying start. After all, just like our children, our dogs are part of our families, and it's only natural to want everyone to get along swimmingly.

If you are planning on getting a pup, you should put in the groundwork before bringing him home. You can educate your children on how the new family member should be approached and to be extra careful not to make loud noises or sudden movements in the early days.

It's a great part of your child's education to teach them about respecting boundaries, and that goes for those of your Tibetan Terrier pup too. It's hugely important to tell children that no matter how adorable your new puppy is, it is not a plaything. A Tibetan Terrier's attitude towards humans very much depends on how the children first communicate with the dog.

Although it's easy to think that a pup has the onus to adapt to the family, Tibetan

FUN FACT
Technically not Terriers

Despite their name, Tibetan Terriers aren't actually terriers. Unlike true terriers, who were bred to hunt rodents and small game, Tibetan Terriers were bred as companion animals and likely received the name terrier due to their small size.

Terriers need consistent and disciplined training to ensure they don't develop bad habits. If confronted by small children behaving in a particularly boisterous way, your Tibetan Terrier may learn to be frightened of kids. Fear manifests as aggression in dogs, irrespective of breed.

When you bring your pup home, get the kids involved in the daily dog-care routine. Personally speaking, when my kids were very young, we made a daily occasion of taking our beloved dog to the woods, and consequently, they both grew up with a strong sense of responsibility in this regard.

Photo Courtesy of Nicky Smith

Perhaps most importantly, your small children should observe the expression "let sleeping dogs lie." When your Tibetan Terrier is sleeping, he should not be disturbed. This also goes for interfering with a puppy while he's eating, as dogs can have an instinctive aggressive response if they feel their food supply is being challenged.

Before you bring your TT home, it is wise to set some ground rules for your kids so that they understand how to respect and care for the new addition to the family. I would advise using positive reinforcement rather than laying down a list of things NOT to do. Here are some suggestions:

- Instead of telling your kids not to shout around your dog, tell them to use quiet voices because it keeps your TT calm and happy.
- Rather than telling your kids not to poke, squeeze, or pull their TT around, let them know that the dog will respond really well to gentle stroking.
- Tell your kids to always wait until their TT comes to them, rather than seeking them out to pick them up. This will build a trustful relationship between your Tibetan Terrier and your children while encouraging your children to respect boundaries.
- Explain to your children that their TT needs personal space for sleeping and eating, just as they do. It's important for the whole family's safety for kids to understand that there are areas in the house reserved especially for your TT.

*Photo Courtesy
of Deborah Stevenson*

First Introductions

Here are some useful tips for the very first time you introduce your children to your new Tibetan Terrier:

Photo Courtesy of Julie Boncher

- Have your child calmly approach your TT from the side, stopping with enough room to allow the dog to willingly greet them. This lets your TT observe your child without feeling overwhelmed or threatened.

- You should keep your TT on its leash while making first introductions to your children. Even if they are a puppy, it is important to start as you mean to continue, and using a leash will give you more control as you introduce your children to them.

- Avoid giving treats or using toys during the first introduction. TTs are easily distracted by the sight of a chew toy—and treats—and they might snatch it from a child's fingers, causing them harm.

- Before your child pets your new TT, let your dog give them a good sniff. Sense of smell is really important to Tibetan Terriers as it tells them so much about what is going on in their surroundings.

- Tell your kids to be careful when offering their hands for your TT to smell. Make sure they curl in their fingers and avoid pushing their hand into the dog's face with a sharp movement.

- If you have a new baby to introduce to the dog, you can give your TT one of their blankets beforehand, so they begin to recognize your baby's scent.

- Observe your TT's body talk during any introductions to children. If they take on a rigid stance, they should be approached with caution, as your TT is telling you that they are not sure if they are ready to greet them.

- Make sure you are present when you introduce your new TT to your children. This introduction should never take place unattended for obvious reasons. Even the best-mannered dogs will respond aggressively if they are hurt, even accidentally. You want to be sure your children don't get bitten at the first meeting, which could irreparably damage your relationship with your TT going forward.

Introducing Your Pup to Other Pets

Although you will naturally want your existing pets and your new Tibetan Terrier pup to get along like a house on fire, it is rarely straightforward. After all, your cat is hardly likely to greet a baby canine with unbridled joy; quite the opposite is often true, in fact!

Young puppies can seem threatening to existing pets, who might be used to getting oodles of attention. Animals can always sense when they are dealing with a baby of a species, and to some degree, that may moderate any aggression, but jealousy could be bubbling, so stay alert.

Generally speaking, it takes around six months for cats and dogs or dogs and dogs to achieve a healthy relationship with each other. When you introduce any new animal into your fold, you must have patience!

Here are some ways you can ease the tension when introducing your Tibetan Terrier pup to other pets:

- Keep your puppy in one area of the house that is completely separate from where you feed your other animals or where there are litter boxes and caged pets. You should be able to shut a door (or cage) so that the puppy can't wander around the house causing chaos.

- If you have pets in cages such as hamsters, chinchillas, etc., take your pup into the same room with them after he has been fed and exercised. This will ensure he is relaxed in the environment and less likely to be conscious of the caged animal near him. Bring your pup's favorite mat and a chew toy so that he recognizes the room as a place to rest.

- In the early days of your new arrival, spoil your resident pets so that they don't feel put out by your adorable Tibetan baby. It's important that your pup sees that there is a pecking order in the pack, particularly as Tibetan Terriers have an innate sense of entitlement in this department! Feed existing pets first. Greet them first. Play with them first. (And don't worry, you won't hurt your TT's feelings.)

- Older dogs are unlikely to be happy about the idea of sharing their space with a new Tibetan Terrier puppy, no matter how cute the pup is. Introduce them on neutral territory like an open field or empty parking lot, or take your older dog to greet the newcomer outside the home. Only take your puppy into your home when the older dog has fully accepted him.

- When introducing your puppy to cats, success will depend on your cat's temperament. Cats are much more inscrutable than even Tibetan

Terriers are, so you have to let them take the lead. Place your pup in an enclosed space such as a crate, and let your cat wander around the room and satisfy its curiosity in the way cats do.

● Cats are unlikely to start the trouble with a pup unless they feel directly threatened. It's an advantage that your Tibetan Terrier may not have seen a cat before, as he is less likely to respond aggressively. In fact, both your cat and your pup will have a mutual curiosity that should consist of little more than sniffing each other out. The trick is to give your cat the upper hand when making the introduction.

Creating a Dedicated Space for Your Tibetan Terrier

> **"**
>
> *Tibetans are natural climbers, having come from the mountains of Tibet. They like to be high off the ground, able to keep an eye on their entire domain. Have a safe space for your TT puppy to play and sleep.*
>
> RENE' STAMM
> *Euphoria Tibetans*
>
> **"**

One of the reasons humans have such rewarding relationships with dogs is because we have more in common than we realize. Just like people, your Tibetan Terrier needs somewhere in your home where he can go to unwind and clear his thoughts.

Tibetan Terriers need to have somewhere where they can let out their frustrations with a solid chewing session or even to run around in circles as Tibetan Terriers tend to do when agitated. Make sure your house is arranged so that there is one zone that only contains things your pup can destroy without causing any upset. Think of it as the equivalent of a man-cave or craft room and pack the area with chew toys and perhaps an indestructible dog bed.

Corners and recesses are really popular with Tibetan Terriers. They feel more secure when they are positioned close to a wall as they get a sense of being protected. If you can only manage a corner as a dedicated space for your pup, make it look inviting rather than a place the dog is sent to as a punishment.

Another good reason for creating a personal space for your Tibetan Terrier is that he'll have somewhere to go if you have visitors to your home. Although Tibetan Terriers absolutely thrive on human company, they can get a little carried away when someone new enters the house. You can make things easier for yourself by having somewhere your pup can relax while you greet guests.

Clear Your Home of Potential Hazards

> *TTs like to be up high. They love to climb and jump. They are like mountain goats. They love to sit up on the top of the back of the couches to look out the windows and see what's going on. They also like to nap on the kitchen counter or in the kitchen sink, like a cat. Just make sure all your meals are where they can't reach them!*
>
> NIKKIE KINZIGER
> *Ri Lee Kennels*

One thing you have to prepare for when you bring ANY pup into your home is the dog's potential for being destructive. Dogs can also cause considerable unintentional damage to themselves unless you ensure there are no hazards in your home. Tibetan Terrier pups are brimming with energy and curiosity, and they will investigate every inch of your home they are allowed entry into. For that reason, you need to make sure your puppy can't get himself into any trouble!

Let's take a closer look at the kind of hazards you need to take care of before you bring your Tibetan Terrier home:

- Some houseplants can be toxic to dogs, such as philodendrons, azaleas, and dieffenbachia, and they will need to be placed out of reach or replaced with nontoxic plants.
- Ensure any medications, including supplements for your pets, are kept in a safe area out of reach of your pup.
- Ensure trash cans in bathrooms are out of reach or that the area is out of bounds to your Tibetan Terrier. The hazards here are sanitary supplies and used razors.

- Be careful when filling sinks and bathtubs with water as they can be a drowning hazard. Also, make sure toilet lids are kept down as puppies have a tendency to drink out of the bowl.

- Store cleaning products in high cupboards or use childproofing on lower cupboards. Also, be careful when using cleaning products around the home, as sprays and vapors can be toxic to your Tibetan Terrier.

- Be mindful of your Tibetan Terrier pup around your furniture. Curiosity can lead him into all sorts of places, such as an open recliner or sofa bed.

- All electrical cords and cables should be out of the puppy zone, as they're very chewable.

- Dangling cords for drapes and blinds are enormous fun for your puppy, but they come with distinct dangers like strangulation.

- Make sure your puppy can't get hold of small items of clothing like socks, nylons, and underwear that have strayed from the laundry basket (or never made it there).

- Keep all small items such as coins, needles, dental floss, paper clips, toys, etc., out of your puppy's reach.

- Use baby gates to separate your puppy from off-limit areas.

- Ensure external doors and windows are closed and securely fastened to prevent escape.

- If you have a cat, make sure your Tibetan Terrier can't get to the litter box. Dogs have a tendency to eat cat feces, which is very dangerous to their health.

- Some human foods are toxic to dogs, such as chocolate, onions, and foods high in salt, fat, or sugar. Ensure your pup is not able to access any of these food products to avoid significant damage to his kidneys, nervous system, and heart.

Prepare Outside Spaces

Your Tibetan Terrier puppy is going to be brimming over with curiosity when he first arrives in your home. Your outside areas are just as much part of your new pup's territory as the inside, so it's worth preparing spaces ahead of his arrival.

With Tibetan Terriers, you need to keep something very important in mind. When they get bored or feel neglected, they can cause an incredible amount of havoc both inside and outside your home.

TTs are known for their nuisance barking, chewing, and digging, but these bad behaviors are generally triggered by boredom or lack of human contact. You'll need to keep your TT properly cared for and exercised daily if you want to keep the damage to a minimum!

Here are a few tips for making your outside spaces safe:

- Make sure there is a fenced-in area where your puppy can play.

- Never leave your pup unattended when outside because he will, without doubt, find—or create—an escape route. An outdoor kennel with secure fencing that your puppy can't dig under or jump over will help contain your Tibetan Terrier's curiosity. Placing rocks at the base of the fence line will make it uncomfortable for them to stand on and will help prevent your TT from digging beneath it.

- Provide a completely separate area that your pup can use as his bathroom. If you have outdoor toys for your children, such as sandboxes or swing sets, make sure your pup can't make messes around them.

- As with houseplants, some of your outdoor plants may be toxic to dogs. Flowers like foxgloves, lilies of the valley, and bulb plants like daffodils are all poisonous to dogs, and landscaping stone can cause intestinal blockages if chewed.

- Ensure that all gardening products like fertilizers, insecticides, and auto supplies, such as antifreeze, are kept in secure places well out of the reach of your Tibetan Terrier.

- If you're lucky enough to have a pool, pond, or hot tub, make sure they are fenced off or covered when not in use. Always prevent your pup from drinking pool water to avoid toxic chemicals.

- Firepits and barbecues are potential hazards for your puppy when in use, so keep them in mind if you're playing host in your garden.

- Ensure all garbage and compost is secured in closed containers.

- Before you welcome your puppy home, take a walk around your property to see if there are any other areas or items that could be hazardous to him, like broken glass or exposed nails, etc.

- Make a plan as to how you will restrict your puppy from access to play areas or hazards so that you're prepared for anything!

Photo Courtesy of Emily Cohen

Ho to Choose a Vet before Your
Tibetan Terrier Gets Home

Choosing the right vet for your Tibetan Terrier is something to be carefully considered. This is someone you are going to have a long relationship with and who could potentially save your TT's life at some point in the future. Here are some tips to help you make a considered choice:

- Ask for personal recommendations: Friends and family members who already have dogs can point you in the right direction for a good local veterinarian. That way, you get first-hand recommendations from people you trust.

- Find a vet specializing in canine health: Not all vets have the same areas of specialty. You will want to work with a vet who understands your Tibetan Terrier and any genetic health conditions they may be predisposed to.

- Check for licenses: It's easy to assume a vet is licensed if they have a physical office, but this is not always the case. Make sure the vet you take your Tibetan Terrier to and any other qualified staff working for the practice are licensed in your state. This will ensure you have full recourse should there be any problem further down the line.

- Ask about the vet's approach to Tibetan Terriers and medicine: The responsibility of a vet extends beyond administering medication. They are also invaluable in planning prevention strategies for health conditions TTs may be vulnerable to.

- Consider the location: You ideally need your vet to be located within a short drive of your home. You want to know you can get to each other quickly should your Tibetan Terrier require urgent attention.

- Count the cost: Vets can vary wildly in how much they charge for their services, and expensive doesn't necessarily mean better! See if a vet's

HELPFUL TIP
TTCA Rescue and Breeder Database

The Tibetan Terrier Club of America (TTCA) operates a nationwide rescue program for TTs. To take part in this program, you'll need to complete a rescue questionnaire on the TTCA website, after which the rescue will contact you whenever a dog is available for adoption in your area. The TTCA also maintains a breeder referral list by state, available to the public on its website.

prices are workable with your budget before you make any commitment to them.

- Make sure everyone gets along: It's vital that you and your Tibetan Terrier are completely comfortable around your vet. Any initial discomfort your TT experiences is likely to make them reluctant to visit in the future. Tibetan Terriers can be extremely stubborn, and if they don't like the look of someone, they will simply refuse to engage with them. (That's a characteristic that's as cute as it is frustrating at times!)

- Look for a clean practice: It's a good idea to pay a visit to your vet's facility and check the level of cleanliness. After all, it is a medical facility, and so it should be as clinically clean as you would expect a human's hospital to be.

CHAPTER 4
Welcoming Home Your Tibetan Terrier

Coping with the Ride Home

Aside from all the preparations to your home and outside spaces before bringing home your TT, you have to navigate the very first journey from the breeder or shelter to your home! This is one of the many things inexperienced dog owners fail to consider, and I say that only because I was one of them. The first journey home can be fraught with danger unless you have a strategy in place beforehand.

Even the most confident dogs can feel easily scared and confused when a new owner takes them home. This is the main reason it is important to get to know your dog before making the journey home so that it's not such a frightening experience for him. Before you get in the car, take some time to sit with your Tibetan Terrier and give him comfort.

Speak in gentle, soothing tones, and if you have chosen a name already, use it when talking to the dog. Forget about establishing yourself as leader of the pack for now; just let your TT take everything in his own stride. Don't make sudden movements or loud noises, and if the dog accidentally pees on you because of nervousness, don't acknowledge it as negative behavior.

Just imagine how huge and intimidating you look

FUN FACT
First American Tibetan Terrier

The first Tibetan Terrier was brought to America in 1956 by an obstetrician, gynecologist, and surgeon named Dr. Henry Murphy and his wife Alice Murphy of Great Falls, Virginia. This black and white female dog was named Gremlin Cortina. Tibetan Terriers were first recognized by the American Kennel Club in 1973 and are currently the 96th most popular breed in the United States.

to this little dog. In the same way as children, TTs feel more secure when approached at their level. Sit down or even lie down and focus your energy on bonding with your new best friend. Hand-feeding your Tibetan Terrier while you are sitting close to him is a great way of breaking the ice. But don't

Photo Courtesy of Alison Boaz

overdo the treats, as you can very quickly set the wrong precedents with ultra-clever Tibetan Terriers at any age.

Hopefully, your pup or rescue Tibetan Terrier will be fine riding in your car, but you can't be sure. Lots of dogs get carsick, so it's worth taking extra towels and garbage bags if you need to change any bedding on the way home. Bring some water in a container to clean up with if the dog makes a mess during the journey.

Take some extra water and a drinking bowl, particularly if you have a long journey. Another thing to bear in mind is the temperature inside your car. If it's cold outside, it might be tempting to make it too warm inside the car to keep the little fellow warm. But ideally, you should keep the temperature at around room temperature so that your Tibetan Terrier transitions easily into your home environment. Make sure that there is good airflow in your car.

Ideally, you should use a crate to contain your Tibetan Terrier when in the car. This will help him feel more secure in a strange environment. As mentioned before, Tibetan Terriers tend to gravitate towards corners and recesses to relax and sleep in. Create a nice space for your new friend to travel home in, preferably with some bedding that already has his scent on it, which you might be able to get from the breeder or shelter.

Depending on how long the journey is, you might want to stop and feed your dog at the halfway point. If you have rescued your Tibetan Terrier, ask the shelter to give you a portion of what they've been feeding the dog for the journey home. If you have a small puppy, he might need to stop more often, as Tibetan Terriers need to eat little and often when they are young. Whatever the dog's age, do NOT overfeed while in transit, as the repercussions can be very unpleasant!

Your Tibetan Terrier

It is important that your TT can't distract you while you're driving. Drivers should have full control of the vehicle at all times, which is difficult unless you have your Tibetan Terrier safely contained.

Because Tibetan Terriers are on the small end of the medium-sized dog scale, it is vital they are secured in a vehicle using either a harness, dog seat belt, or a transport crate. If left to their own devices or attached by a long enough leash, they will cause havoc in the back while you are driving.

If you use a harness or seat belt, ensure that they are a snug fit without too much 'give' in them. Make sure your TT is able to comfortably sit or lie

Photo Courtesy of Renè Stamm

down while secured but that there isn't enough leeway for them to move very far from their spot. The idea is to make sure your TT can't be thrown around the car as you turn corners or take bends and especially if you were to have an accident.

Transport crates are often recommended for Tibetan Terrier puppies, as you'll be able to get them used to it more easily than an adult. Unless your adult Tibetan Terrier is used to using a crate and associates it with relaxation and sleep, it's unwise to introduce one when they're older.

The main consideration with a transport crate is how to secure it in your vehicle. Fortunately, due to a TT's size, you can position the crate more or less where you want as long as it is placed so that it cannot possibly move when you set off. Use seat belts to secure the crate if you're placing it on the back seat and straps if your TT is traveling in the trunk.

Supplies to Have Ready

Your house should be already puppy-proofed and outside spaces secured by the time you get home, and there are supplies you need to have ready from day one. Here are some of those items, which you should purchase before you bring your Tibetan Terrier home.

Dog crate: If you have purchased or rescued a puppy, there's a very good chance he has not been housebroken. Crate training has become a hugely popular way of helping dogs learn how to be clean and where and when to use the bathroom. Tibetan Terriers generally enjoy a crated lifestyle because they feel safe and secure in smaller spaces rather than a dedicated room. You should get a crate that your TT can use when it is fully grown so that it really becomes the dog's home. You can always make a crate feel smaller for a pup by padding it with towels and cushions. Tibetan Terriers have a strong appreciation for anything luxurious! To find out more about crate training, see Chapter 6.

Dog bed: It goes without saying that the quality of your Tibetan Terrier's bed is a BIG DEAL. It's worth investing in a chew-proof dog bed if possible, but the most important thing is size. Yes, size matters when it comes to choosing the right bed for your Tibetan Terrier. They like a tight fit, which often means they curl up and go to sleep in the most unexpected places! Your dog bed should fit in the crate if you have one, and if not, the bed shouldn't be too large.

Feeding and Water Bowls: Obviously, your Tibetan Terrier will need to drink or eat soon after arriving at your home. You'll need to have the right kind of food bowls on hand. Although it sounds like an easy decision, bowls can slide all over the floor, flip-up, break, and create all kinds of messes unless they're a good design. I usually go for stainless steel, which cleans easily, but there are also some really good plastic bowls that are water-cooled, which are handy if you live in a warm climate as I do.

Dog food: As already mentioned, you can easily set a precedent with a Tibetan Terrier. In other words, they become accustomed to things very quickly, which I discovered at some expense! Don't assume that more expensive dog food is going to be the best choice for your TT; the nutritional value is what you need to consider. Think about whether you will feed your dog wet or dry food, and make sure whatever you get is suitable for their age. Puppy food is generally specially formulated for young dogs, as they have different nutritional requirements than adult Tibetan Terriers. There's more information about the TT's nutritional requirements in Chapter 8.

*Photo Courtesy
of Andrea Read*

Items for walkies: You'll need a dog collar, leash or harness, and poop bags and holder (or fanny pack as I use). Although TTs don't require quite as much paraphernalia as a young child, you still need to be prepared before you head out on your first walk with him. Make a decision as to whether you will use a harness or traditional collar and lead and make sure everything is adjustable! This is important because your Tibetan Terrier pup will grow at a fairly rapid rate in the early months.

ID tag: If your Tibetan Terrier has not been microchipped, you should ensure your vet does this as soon as possible. It is also a good idea to have visual information on your dog's collar by way of an ID tag. This is mainly because microchips have to be scanned in order to determine the owner, whereas a tag will tell people who to contact immediately should your Tibetan Terrier wander off.

Dog toys: Tibetan Terriers are really playful, even when they are fully grown, and they love nothing more than interacting with humans. You can't fail to entertain your Tibetan Terrier with games, especially if you're playing them too. However, you haven't got all day, and so it's important to stock up with dog toys that will amuse your Tibetan Terrier when you have other things to do. Puzzle toys engage their curiosity, chew toys prevent them from chewing your things, and chase toys are great for getting them to run around and exercise.

Grooming brushes: This is very important for a Tibetan Terrier because of their unique layered coat and its tendency for matting. You'll be surprised quite how quickly a TT's long overcoat grows. Grooming is a really soothing experience for Tibetan Terriers, and it will help your dog adjust to your home quickly if you introduce a brushing schedule from day one.

Other doggie products: Dog toothpaste and toothbrush, flea and tick collars, and shampoo should all be on your list of supplies to purchase before you welcome your Tibetan Terrier home.

Household cleaning products: Trust me, Tibetan Terriers get into all kinds of mischief when they're exploring a new environment. They have an insatiable and often destructive curiosity, so you need to be prepared. Have some enzyme spray and carpet cleaner ready for any accidents your Tibetan Terrier has.

If you're a newbie dog owner, ask friends and other family members with dogs for any recommendations for vets, dog groomers, or a dog sitter they swear by so that you have a head start in making the right connections. Find out where the best dog parks are close by so that you can get your TT socialized. One thing a Tibetan Terrier loves more than anything is being the center of your attention at all times, and you might need outside help!

The First Nights

> **"**
>
> *While you may want your TT to sleep by themselves, but it generally doesn't make for a quiet night. Place the crate right next to your bed, and let your magic hand sooth an anxious puppy. Tapping lightly on the top of the crate reminds your puppy that you are there with them. That's all that is needed. You can move the crate further away in a week or two, into a permanent corner of the bedroom.*
>
> JACKIE FAUST
> *Arkeden Tibetan Terriers*
> **"**

Your Tibetan Terrier will feel more secure in his new environment if he gets settled into a bedtime routine from the start. Consistency is key with all puppy training, as was proven by Russian physiologist Ivan Pavlov, which we'll cover in more depth in a later chapter.

You should have already decided where your puppy will be sleeping before bringing your Tibetan Terrier home. Whether you are okay with him sleeping in your bedroom or want him to have a dedicated area, you should decide which way to go and stick with it.

For example, if you start your puppy off sleeping in your bedroom but decide at a later date that it's not working out, it can cause your Tibetan Terrier distress. As instinctive animals, a dog's sleeping area and also where it feeds are integral to its need for a territory. If dogs are constantly being shunted around from room to room, they will quickly become confused and stressed, which could lead to behavioral problems.

Remain calm whenever you are with your new Tibetan Terrier but especially when it's time for bed. Give the dog gentle strokes as you praise him while he settles into the special space you have created just for him. Be prepared to stick around for a while on the first night, as your Tibetan Terrier will have already made a connection with YOU but not as much with your home.

You may want to sleep in the same room you have chosen for your TT pup if it is not your bedroom. You have to keep in mind that not only is your puppy adjusting to new surroundings but also from being apart from his mother. Just imagine the human equivalent of a newborn baby, and you can imagine how distressing this might be for the dog.

If you are able to grab a blanket or toy from the breeder or shelter that already carries your Tibetan Terrier's scent, put this in his sleeping spot, and it will help comfort him. Remember that it is OK to comfort your Tibetan Terrier, no matter what age he is. If he becomes anxious in the night, you should be quick to give him a comforting stroke or cuddle. Showing anxiety and stress is a natural response to being thrust into new surroundings and is not negative behavior that needs addressing.

Getting into a Routine

> *Tibetans do best with families that have previous dog experience or those that can set guidelines/boundaries for their dog and actually stick with them. Routine in a TTs life makes for a better behaved and well-adjusted dog.*
>
> RENE' STAMM
> *Euphoria Tibetans*

Dogs of all breeds simply LOVE routines! They feel secure when they know what is taking place around them and draw comfort from repeated behaviors. If you consider how your own daily routine keeps you grounded, it is the same for your Tibetan Terrier. You can create your TT's routines around your own, such as feeding the dog as you get ready for work and leaving the house at the same time each day.

If you work shifts or have unscheduled working hours, think of a phrase you can repeat before you leave home every morning. For example, say to your TT, "I'm just off to work now, and I will see you later." Just say the phrase every time you leave for work without any further fuss or attention to your Tibetan Terrier. He will very quickly learn to associate the phrase with an idea of how long you are likely to be gone, and even if he doesn't like it, he will learn to accept this pattern of activity.

When you have a Tibetan Terrier puppy, you should introduce routines for sleeping, eating, and using the bathroom in dedicated places and at consistent times. It won't be long before he follows the routine on automatic pilot. Tibetan Terriers are quick learners when they have consistent and motivated training.

The Art of Easy Housetraining

Tibetan Terriers are extremely intelligent, which makes training less arduous than it can be for other breeds. The first training obstacle to overcome is housetraining. Here are some tips for making this easier for yourself. Depending on your training efforts, housetraining can be achieved in as little as a week to as long as 3-4 months. By patiently following these steps, you can have your TT housetrained within the shortest period of time.

1 Your TT pup is tiny and can't possibly want to use the bathroom that much? Well, you're about to get the shock of your life! For the first few weeks in your home, it will seem that your pup needs to eliminate every time it is active. This is not unusual. Tibetan Terrier pups need to learn bladder and bowel control in just the same way as humans do.

2 Don't let your TT pup wander around your home unless supervised. If you keep your pup in its bed or crate when you are busy elsewhere, you can prevent accidents in the wrong places.

3 If you see your TT sniffing the ground and walking in circles, quickly take them to the desired 'pooping' area because elimination is imminent. Always praise your TT when they have pooped in the correct place. They simply adore being in your good books!

4 Never get angry if your puppy has made a mess in the wrong place. This will have a detrimental effect on your housetraining. Under no circumstances 'rub their nose in it,' as this will do nothing but confuse and upset them.

5 Take care not to overfeed your pup as they may need to eliminate more than usual. Feed them the same measured amounts at the same time of day, and when they walk away, remove the bowl.

6 Keep in mind that puppies instinctively need to eliminate after eating, drinking, playing, resting, sleeping, or if they've been left alone for a while. Five to thirty minutes after any of these activities, take your TT to where they can use the toilet.

7 Use one specific verbal cue that it's time for your dog to do their business, like "go potty." If you use the same cue every time, your TT will quickly associate the cue with the required action.

8 When they start to eliminate, begin to praise them quietly, and when they're done, ramp it up and give them a treat immediately. If they are unable to eliminate, take them back to their bed or crate and try again in another 15 minutes.

Photo Courtesy of Helen Baker

9 It's important to remember that you have responsibility for preventing accidents. Your TT is totally in your hands when it comes to housetraining, and they are inherently eager to please. Any accidents should be thoroughly cleaned without acknowledgment that your TT has done anything wrong. Just as we say to our children, Tibetan Terriers need to know that 'accidents happen.'

10 Prevent accidents as much as you can by becoming aware of how often your TT needs to eliminate. When they are puppies, they are likely to need to go outside every 30 to 60 minutes.

11 Finally, reward with praise every time, but as your TT learns where and when to use the bathroom, reduce the food rewards. You will make a rod for your own back if you always give in to your TT with treats, mark my words!

Counting the Costs of Your Tibetan Terrier

Tibetan Terriers come with price tags that go way beyond the original expense of paying a breeder or making a shelter donation. There are several expenses that you'll want to budget for if you have chosen to invite a TT into your life. Vet fees, training costs, food and other supplies, grooming, etc., can all add up to considerable sums of money!

Here is a chart showing the approximate expenses involved when you first take your TT home:

Necessities	Costs
Puppy Food	$85
Dog Treats	$25
Crate	$65
Toys	$60
Bed	$30
Bowls, Leash, and Miscellaneous	$60
Carpet Cleaner, Waste Bag	$45
Initial Vaccines	$115
Initial Vet Consultation	$55
Deworming, Flea and Tick Meds	$20
Dog License	$20
TOTAL	**$620**

And here's another showing the average monthly costs involved in owning an adult Tibetan Terrier from 2 years upwards.

Necessities	Costs
Food	$85
Treats	$25
Health Insurance	$30-$50
Toys	$12
Medications	$32
Miscellaneous Supplies	$15
TOTAL	**$169+**

Naturally, the above costs are not set in stone and depend very much on your budget and availability. However, they are a very good rule of thumb estimate as to how much your TT will set you back on an annual basis. Of course, you'll be the first to know Tibetan Terriers are worth every cent!

CHAPTER 5

Are You Ready for Puppy Parenthood?

> "
>
> *TTs love 'their' people and are usually thrilled to accompany them anywhere! An active lifestyle is great, but this breed is also happy to relax on the couch with you.*
>
> MAUREEN DWYER
> *Yonpo Tibetan Terriers*
> "

Tibetan Terriers: Expectation vs. Reality

You'll have an easier time raising a puppy or accepting an adult Tibetan Terrier into your home if you keep your expectations firmly in reality. It's vital that you have a good idea of what a TT is capable of at any given point in its development and how proactive you'll have to be in ensuring good behavior.

Here's a list of common misconceptions people have about Tibetan Terriers (especially as pups) versus the reality:

1. Snuggle Time

The Expectation: With a Tibetan Terrier's enchanting looks, it's easy to imagine lots of snuggle time. Many dream of a TT curling up by their side as they run their hands through that magnificent coat.

The Reality: In reality, when you want to snuggle your TT pup, he'll probably be more interested in using you as a chew toy. Of course, there will be time to snuggle, but it's usually best to leave that until the end of the day before it's time for bed!

Adult Tibetan Terriers are likely to be more accommodating, and they love nothing more than being as close to your side as possible. That said, they can become overly obsessed with being around you, and you need to ensure your dog doesn't become anxious whenever he's left alone. (See Chapter 7 for more information on separation anxiety.)

Photo Courtesy of Amanda Green

2. Puppy Proofing

The Expectation: People often think that the size of a Tibetan Terrier pup doesn't really pose much of a threat to your home. Even when fully grown, you'll look into those gorgeous dark eyes (if you can see them, of course) and ask yourself: "How much trouble can this little guy possibly get into?" People with this rose-tinted view of their new TT can reject the idea of crates, baby gates, and exercise pens for being unnecessary, which is often to their detriment!

The Reality: Tibetan Terriers are incredibly bright and full of curiosity. Naturally, these traits are amplified when they are puppies exploring the world for the first time. Your TT will find objects to chew or destroy that you weren't even aware of being in your home. If you think a valued artifact is safe from the paws of your adorable TT, it almost certainly isn't!

Until you have trained your TT pup or retrained a rescue adult, he will probably have a go at anything that isn't nailed to the floor of your home. When left to their own devices, TT pups, in particular, can pull at threads in your rug, chew electrical cables, chomp on table legs, and destroy scatter cushions in a matter of minutes.

To prevent this kind of behavior, you need to provide some great dog toys for your TT. Don't go overboard as he will get bored easily, so you want

Photo Courtesy of Lucas Davis

to let him have access to three or four toys at the same time and rotate them with others while they get cleaned. TT pups, in particular, respond with huge excitement when they see a familiar toy, so it's worth hiding those toys every once in a while.

Another tip that's useful for any age TT is to interact as much as possible with him when the dog decides its playtime. Very often, TTs will chew things only as a means of getting attention. If you play with them using their own doggie toys, they will learn to bring you one of those when they want your attention instead.

3. Exercise

The Expectation: Prospective TT owners often expect long walks that will help them get out and exercise more too. However, there are different things to expect from adult and puppy Tibetan Terriers.

The Reality: If you have a puppy TT, you should not try and take him for a walk as you would an adult. Puppy needs are completely different, and so your expectations should be too. Take time on your first walk with your TT pup, as it's a major life experience for him! Sit with your dog outside your home for around 15-20 minutes, or carry him to an outside space where he can just take in the new sights, sounds, and smells. Avoid trying to walk your TT formally on the first adventure outside, but on the second attempt, you can start introducing some leash training sessions using these four tips:

Photo Courtesy of Neil Ravey

- Short sessions: Keep your leash training to just 5-10 minutes. Even during this short time, your TT can learn a great deal. Remember, he'll still be adjusting to the world around him.

- Take some boiled chicken or a tug toy so you can show your TT how much fun it is to engage with you while on a leash.

- Lots of TT pups will simply "lock-up" while out on walks, which means they'll just refuse to budge. Never be tempted to drag or pull your dog when he does this. Tibetan Terriers can be hugely stubborn, and they will dig in their heels. Just stop for as long as your pup wants to absorb everything he's experiencing and take things at his pace.

- Bear in mind your pup will not walk as quickly or for as long as an adult TT. He will want to walk much more slowly while sniffing everything he encounters and picking up the odd leaf or twig. These deeply curious dogs will want to examine every inch of the outside world in the early days of leash training.

4. Jumping

The Expectation: You arrive home, and as you cross the threshold, your TT runs enthusiastically to you and jumps up to be lifted into your arms. This will melt even the hardest of hearts, and so it's with delight that you

Photo Courtesy of Alison Simmons

see your TT behaving the same way with visiting friends and family. "Look at how much he LOVES everyone!" Even when out on walks, your TT displays the same level of affection for everyone he encounters, and you can't imagine that it could ever be a problem. It's easy to dismiss this kind of behavior as something your pup will grow out of.

The Reality: If you have a TT pup, you should know that he will get better and better at every behavior he practices. As with humans, habits—good or bad—are developed by repeating a certain behavior, and it's the same for TTs. If you don't curb your dog's tendency to jump up at you and other people, he will continue to accost everyone he encounters by jumping up at them. You'll soon discover how unpopular that will make YOU as the person responsible for your TT's behavior.

HELPFUL TIP
Preventing Separation Anxiety

Tibetan Terriers are excellent companion dogs, but how will they behave when you're not around? Because of their affectionate nature, Tibetan Terriers are apt to develop separation anxiety. Puppies can't be left alone for more than an hour or two at a time until they're around six months of age. But as much as you'll want to cuddle and spoil your puppy constantly, there are some early steps that you can take to prevent separation anxiety from becoming an issue later in life. Establishing a routine of crating your puppy while you're present is a great way to decrease your puppy's stress about being crated when you're away.

Similarly, a rescue or adopted adult TT could have developed deep-rooted bad behaviors as a consequence of prior treatment. In the same way as TT pups, these behaviors can be corrected in adults by consistent positive reinforcement, although usually, it takes less time.

If you anticipate when you have visitors or when you will be greeting another person, you can make things easier for yourself. When you take your TT for a walk, take some small treats with you and tell others that your pup is in training or that you are retraining a rescue adult. Encourage calm behavior with treats but don't overdo it as your TT will get accustomed to being fed whenever you walk him!

You can use the same approach when people visit your home to encourage your TT not to jump up at guests. Make sure he doesn't react to your doorbell in a negative way by getting excited; rather, encourage him to go to his bed and wait to be greeted. When people say hello, you want your pup or adult TT to be calm and have all four paws on the ground.

5. The 'Non-Barker'

The Expectation: If you have rescued or adopted an adult TT, you should have found out whether the dog has an issue with barking from the shelter or foster parent. However, with a TT pup, it is very common to be lulled into a false sense of security in the early weeks when the dog isn't very vocal yet.

The Reality: The fun starts when a Tibetan Terrier finds his full voice during adolescence or early adulthood. Although you would think Tibetan Terriers would be yappy as a relatively small breed, they have a surprisingly deep bark. Remember that they worked with herdsmen in Tibet, and so they are instinctively programmed to alert you about strangers.

You want to avoid having your TT make barking a hobby. Tibetan Terriers can sometimes enjoy the sound of their own barking a bit too much! Be firm,

Photo Courtesy of Karen Dean

consistent, and assertive about laying down rules, and in very little time, your TT will not disappoint. (These adorable creatures will do ANYTHING not to disappoint you.)

Whether the dog is a pup or an adult, excessive barking can be a coping strategy for a Tibetan Terrier. Take time to find out what it is that triggers your TT to start barking, and that will help you solve the problem. The subject of excessive barking is covered in more depth in Chapter 7.

Teething Problems

In a perfect world, your TT pup will settle into your home seamlessly and without making any messes or having any accidents. Unfortunately, this is not reality. In the first days, you will have some difficulties adjusting, and some of those may be related to literal teething problems a puppy will have.

Just like human babies, TT pups are born without teeth. When they are around three to four weeks old, their first set of baby or milk teeth will start to grow. At the age of four or five months, your Tibetan Terrier's milk teeth will fall out to make room for a permanent set. By five to seven months, the pup will have a full set of adult teeth.

In other words, your TT pup will experience teething twice in the early months of development—once for his milk teeth and again for his adult teeth. Although your puppy doesn't feel major pain during this process, he can feel some discomfort in his jaw. When you realize that the teeth actually cut through the gum as they emerge, it's easy to understand that it is not a pleasant experience.

The best way to reduce your pup's discomfort is also the same way we deal with human babies' teething troubles. Give your TT some specially designed chew toys for teething that are filled with gel. You can put these toys in your deep freeze, and that will act as a numbing agent to reduce any pain as your pup chews away.

The most important thing to understand is that your TT will have an instinctive desire to chew when he is teething. If you don't supply him with plenty of objects designed for the job, he will turn his attention to your furniture!

Here are some of the signs your TT pup is teething:

- His gums are red and inflamed.
- He drools and has bad breath.

*Photo Courtesy
of Kim Pollard*

- There is increased chewing, during which you should provide safe toys and discourage biting.
- There are bleeding gums, which is normal as the teeth emerge through them.
- There are missing teeth, which are usually safely swallowed by your TT when they fall out.
- There is decreased appetite, or your TT takes more time to eat due to discomfort.
- Your TT may whine and fuss more than usual or be a little grumpy, which small children should be made aware of.

You should take your TT pup to a vet if he exhibits any of the following:

- A slight fever is normal, but it should be monitored so that the dog's temperature doesn't climb too high.
- Although there will be blood spotting during teething, if you notice profuse bleeding, you should take your TT to the vet immediately.
- Before your pup's adult teeth have grown in, take him to see your vet for a precautionary checkup.

Whether you have an adult or a puppy Tibetan Terrier, they will both require regular dental checks. Generally, the vet will look at the following in pups and any adults that have been acquired from a shelter or foster parent.

Crooked teeth: When two teeth emerge at the same spot or if a milk tooth has not fallen out before the adult tooth grows in, it can cause crooked teeth.

Jaw misalignment: If your TT shows signs of a strong underbite or overbite, dental intervention may be required to prevent chewing and eating problems in the future.

Bad breath: It is not normal for dogs to have bad breath and generally indicates the possibility of a mild infection.

Broken or cracked teeth: Teeth can break and expose the nerve, particularly if broken below the gum line. This will cause your TT lots of discomfort, and he will risk developing an infection.

Tartar buildup: Although it is unusual for TT pups to have tartar buildup, it does occasionally happen. If you implement a good dental routine in the early days of having your TT home, it can prevent dental diseases in the future. Cleaning teeth is as important as "controlled chewing" for dental health.

Establishing Boundaries

When you first bring your TT home, you will need to waste no time in setting rules, boundaries, and limitations. Your TT really needs to know what he can do, where he can do it, and for how long in order to feel secure with a consistent routine.

Establishing boundaries is vital in solving certain behavior problems, such as your dog getting on the sofa, begging at the dining table, or bolting when a door is opened. In essence, when you create a boundary, you build an invisible barrier and teach your TT not to cross it. Here are some really good tips to help you build boundaries for your Tibetan Terrier.

Claim your space: Like other breeds, Tibetan Terriers instinctively claim their own space when interacting with other dogs. They do it with their body language and energy and are able to communicate a message like "this is mine" without barking, baring their teeth, or growling. A Tibetan Terrier claiming its food bowl, for example, will stand above it while leaning his head down in a protective way.

If another dog wants to claim your TT's space, he will just stride up to the dog and barge right on through. If you want to assert your leadership and claim your space, you'll have to do the same thing with your TT. If you don't want your TT to enter the house, block the doorway so that he can't get in. If you don't want him getting on your couch, stand over it protectively so that your TT will understand your body language.

Take the lead: You need to emphasize to your TT from a very early stage that you are the leader of the pack. A great way of doing this is by creating a rule where your TT allows you to enter a room before him. You can start training him when on-leash, making him stop and wait before the threshold. Once you have stepped into the room, invite your TT to follow. Repeat this exercise several times a day until your TT understands that you go first, and he follows behind.

Teach your dog to wait: If you've already taught your TT a trick such as "paw," then you'll understand that once he has mastered something, he will quickly associate the action with treats. This means that he'll be inclined to get into position whenever he sees you reach for the treats. Although this isn't bad behavior, it's important that you get your TT to respond to your commands and cues only.

If this has happened, it's important to retrain your TT not to perform the trick until he's heard the command, even if you are holding a treat in front of him. When a TT starts to anticipate something, he will often think that performing a trick is what will make you give him the treat. You have to reverse this way of thinking by pulling back treats if he starts to perform, only letting him have the goody when he has responded to your command. This will also teach your TT to look for your signal before deciding on an action and will make for a better relationship between the dog and you and your family.

Correct at the right time: The key to creating boundaries for your TT is in correcting his behavior when he crosses the line. If you are trying to teach your TT not to get on your couch, it doesn't help to correct him while he is already sitting on it. Although extremely bright, TTs are not necessarily fast at connecting the dots, and your dog won't understand why he is being corrected. You need to correct bad behavior before your TT is about to commit an offense. That way, he will connect the correction with the behavior, and he will know exactly what he is doing wrong.

Be consistent: Once you have decided where your TT is and isn't allowed, you will need to be consistent in two areas: maintaining the boundary and allowing for exceptions. If you have made the decision that your TT can join you on the sofa as an occasional treat, make sure it is always at your invitation. This is important in reminding your TT that he is not allowed to invade your space unless he is invited to do so. Your training messages need to be consistent across all members of the household, using the same cues and commands where required. This sounds harsh, but it is really important not to confuse your TT, as that can lead to him becoming anxious and depressed. Or worse, it will make him think that he is the leader of the pack and not you and other members of the household.

CHAPTER 6
Crate Training your Tibetan Terrier

Crate or No Crate?

There are many people who feel a crate confines a dog in a cruel way, although with TTs, this is very much not the case. Tibetan Terriers really like being in spaces not much bigger than they are as it gives them a sense of security. When done properly, crate training is a really effective management system that can be a lifesaver for both you and your TT.

Like any other training method, crating is open to abuse, but when used correctly and for appropriate time periods, it can help you achieve important goals such as housetraining, preventing destructive behavior, and teaching your TT when it is time to relax.

As with all other aspects of training, if your TT is taught through positive reinforcement to enjoy being in his crate, it will soon become his own. The crate will become a safe haven for your TT and will be a place he can go when he doesn't want to be disturbed. All breeds of dog have a natural instinct to den, and the majority take to crate training very well.

HELPFUL TIP
How Smart Are They?

Tibetan Terriers are intelligent dogs who are eager to please. With positive reinforcement and consistent training, Tibetan Terriers should be quick to learn new tricks and commands.

There are a number of benefits crate training brings to owners. You should ensure your TT's crate is sized properly (read more about size below), as your Tibetan Terrier already has an instinct not to mess where he sleeps. This natural tendency to view the crate as a clean space is a big benefit when it comes to house-training a new rescue TT or pup.

Using a crate will prevent your TT from getting into trouble when you're not around to supervise him directly. Those times might be at night when you're sleeping, when you're at work, when you're busy cooking, or at any other time when your attention is required elsewhere. One thing to bear in mind is if you have to leave your TT alone for long hours, he will need to exercise before you leave and when you return.

Crate training is invaluable in teaching excitable TTs to enjoy downtime too. You can place your TT in his crate with a yummy treat and a chew toy and leave him to relax. This will also keep the little tyke from creating mischief!

Photo Courtesy of Lucas Davis

Choosing a Crate: Type, Size, and Location

There are many different types of crates available, which can make it a little daunting to figure out the correct size and style for your TT. The most common types of crates are made of wire, plastic, and fabric.

Fabric crates are particularly useful for traveling, sporting events, and camping. You should get your TT used to either a wire or plastic crate before trying out the fabric version. This is mainly because such crates are not as robust and are also not recommended for long periods of time without supervision. However, the advantage of fabric crates is that they are lightweight and can be folded flat for easy storage and travel.

The best crate for your TT to use at home is one made of plastic or wire. Many people favor wire crates as they fold flat for storage in a similar way to the fabric versions. They are also cheaper and more robust than plastic crates. If you are looking for a crate that blends well with your interiors, you can even purchase dog crate furniture combinations that double as end tables! Who knew?

Selecting the correct size crate for your TT can be confusing. Some people choose large size crates to give their TTs plenty of room to move around. However, as mentioned earlier, your TT will want a nice compact space where there isn't the possibility of him using a corner of it as a toilet.

Choose a crate that is just large enough for your TT to stand up, turn around, and lie down comfortably in, at least until he is house-trained. The majority of wire crates come with dividers to allow you to block off an area to allow room for a growing TT. If you have chosen a plastic crate, you can place a box on one side of it to make the usable space smaller. This will prevent you from having to buy multiple crates as your TT pup grows.

FUN FACT
Best in Show

As of 2020, a Tibetan Terrier has not won Best in Show at the annual Westminster Kennel Club Dog Show. Tibetan Terriers are part of the non-sporting group, including a diverse collection of dogs such as bulldogs, Chow Chows, and Lhasa Apsos

The best area of the house to place the crate in is somewhere you and your TT can both access it easily. The crate should be near enough to be on-hand but out of the way enough so that you aren't constantly tripping over it. Placing the crate by the side of your bed when your TT is a pup can help him to sleep more easily, particularly as you will be right beside him.

Introduce Your Tibetan Terrier to His Crate Gradually

It's a better idea to introduce your TT to his crate slowly, rather than just placing him in it for the night or during long periods of your absence. This is particularly distressing for TTs, who have a tendency for separation anxiety (see Chapter 7). When you first bring your TT home, get him used to his crate by tossing in a chew toy or a treat and leaving the door open. Let him sniff around the crate and find his own way in and explore the new environment. When your TT is comfortable going in and out of the crate, toss another treat inside and close the door just for a second or two before letting him out of it.

It helps your TT to become accustomed to his crate if there is an item in it that he is already familiar with. Place a mat or a bed that your TT likes in the crate, and this will help him feel relaxed sooner. When you are not crate training, you can leave the door open and leave treats, toys, and, importantly, your dog's bed inside. This way, your TT will learn that the crate is a fun place that is especially for him if he wants to relax. You can also feed him in the crate, initially leaving the door open and closing it over time as part of the training process.

The idea is to get your TT to associate good things with the crate. You can take the mat or bed with you when visiting the vet.

How to Cue Him In and Out of the Crate

When your TT goes into his crate willingly, add a command or cue for entering, such as "crate" or "bed." Say the command as you toss a treat for your TT into the crate. It won't be long before your TT is happy to get into his crate on cue and without any persuasion!

Once you have set this association in your TT's mind, try giving the crate cue and waiting for him to enter on his own. Stop tossing a treat inside and leave it to your TT to enter when he is cued to. As soon as he enters after your cue, give him lots of praise immediately so that he knows he has behaved as you want him to.

Then you can start training your dog on a release cue. This will tell your TT when he is free to leave his crate. This part of crate training has the additional benefit of encouraging and increasing self-control, which can be an issue with TTs. Your TT will learn to remain calm and not rush out immediately once the door is open.

After you have cued your TT's entrance and praised him for complying, you can say a release cue, like "okay" or "out now," and toss a treat on the floor just outside the crate. Keep tossing treats until your TT leaves the crate without seeing it and responds just on your verbal cue. When you get to this point, you can phase out treats because just leaving the crate and pleasing you has now become your TT's reward.

Photo Courtesy of Sherry Franklyn

Duration

If your TT is relaxed with the crate door closed for a few seconds, you can gradually increase the time he spends in it. Remember to use the same release cue consistently to tell your TT he can leave. If he has a problem remaining in the crate calmly for several minutes, start closing the door and leaving the room for a second or so before returning.

Gradually increase the time your TT is in the crate. If he starts to whine, ignore him and only let him out when he has calmed down. If you respond to your TT every time he shows the slightest distress, he is more likely to develop a nervous disposition, which can manifest as aggression.

A really good rule of thumb to use when determining how long your TT should spend in his crate is one hour for every month of his age. Throughout the whole crate training process, it is vital that you remain patient and don't push your TT. You may well want to speed things up, but it will ultimately make your TT uncomfortable, making crate training much harder.

It is best to take baby steps with your TT's crate training. If you can get him to be relaxed and comfortable in his crate before the first night he spends in it, you are much more likely to get a good night's sleep. Once your TT is completely house and crate trained, you can leave him inside it for up to eight hours. It is very important that you exercise your TT well both before and after spending time in his crate. Don't worry that he'll be bored, as he will more than likely be sleeping without any distractions to hold his attention.

All effective training should be in sync with the stage of your TT's development. One hour for every month of age is sufficient, which means a three-month-old TT can spend three hours inside a crate without any discomfort.

It's really useful for your young TT pup to sleep in his crate at night, as this helps him learn a regular sleeping pattern and also allows you to let him out quickly for a bathroom break. You can place the crate by your bed so that the dog is comforted by being close to you, which is all-important for TTs of any age. Once he is used to sleeping through the night in his crate, you can move it to another dedicated area of your home.

When a Little Extra Is Needed

Although many TTs take to crates with great ease, others can be more reluctant. If your TT whines, cries, or makes a fuss that keeps you awake, it's the most natural thing to release him from the crate and scoop him up into

Photo Courtesy
of Kelli Murphy

bed with you. However, your dog will quickly learn that making a fuss will help him get what he wants. You have to exercise extreme patience if your TT makes a fuss so that you get the message across that calm behavior is the key to opening the crate door!

If you are strong, you will make it through the first few nights with your TT pup. Put things with familiar scents in the crate with your TT so that he knows he is in a secure place. Remember your TT pup will have been used to sleeping with his siblings and mother, and he will very likely be confused by the separation.

Time-out

If you do crate training properly, your TT will be conditioned to relax and settle down once he is inside it. You can also use the crate to correct bad behavior by using it as a time-out zone. You have to be careful with this approach so that you don't confuse your TT, and he becomes nervous about using the crate.

If your TT pup is displaying unwanted behavior, place him into the crate for a few minutes as a time-out. This teaches the dog to settle down and removes all reinforcing stimuli for his "bad" behavior. If you feel you have to resort to putting your TT in a time-out at several points during the day, there's a risk of the dog developing a negative association with the crate, and so you should change your approach. Ideally, using the crate as a method for modifying behavior should be an absolute last resort.

From the Crate Onward

Creating a positive association with the crate is a valuable part of your TT's training. One of the benefits of crate training your TT is that he is likely to be much better at traveling with you, especially if he needs to visit the vet or groomer. When crate trained with positive reinforcement and patience, your TT will be totally relaxed in his dedicated space and will eagerly enter when asked. All you need to do at your end is invest your time—and a few treats along the way—and you'll end up with a happy Tibetan Terrier and happy humans too!

CHAPTER 7

Leaving Your Tibetan Terrier Home Alone for the First Time

When you first bring your TT home, he is likely to be a little anxious, whether he is a puppy or an adult. You need to consider how you can make your TT comfortable when you first have to leave him alone.

It's not just owners of TT pups that face this dilemma, either. New foster or rescue TTs can be just as anxious about being left alone, especially if they have just found a safe space after leaving an abusive background.

Photo Courtesy
of Jess Kenny

Tips for Leaving Your Tibetan Terrier on His Own

1 **LOTS OF EXERCISE BEFOREHAND**

If you are adopting or rescuing an adult TT, give him a long walk at least once a day. Assuming that you and your TT are both fit and healthy, this walk should last for at least 30 minutes and preferably more than an hour. Walking is a bonding ritual for TTs, and it helps a dog get to know a new owner and understand a new routine. Before you leave your new companion alone for the first time, take him for a lovely long walk so that he is relaxed and happy when you leave.

2 **TAKE A DAY OR TWO OFF FROM WORK**

You'll know ahead of time when you're due to bring your TT home. If possible, it's good to take a few days off work so that you can really get to know each other before you have to start leaving the dog for long periods.

During your days off work with your TT, start leaving him at home alone for short periods of time so that he becomes accustomed to being on his own in a new environment.

3 **TAKE BABY STEPS TEACHING YOUR TT TO BE RELAXED ON HIS OWN**

It is never a good idea to leave a TT of any age alone for eight hours right off the bat. Start with just five minutes while you run a quick errand. Then try 10 minutes later on that same day, then 20 minutes, 30 minutes, etc., working up to 45 minutes and then going for an hour.

Even if your TT is just eight weeks old, it is important to start training him to be alone from an early stage. That way, he will adjust to your absence over time and will be less inclined to become anxious. Start by leaving your TT alone for a few minutes while you head off into another room.

It's a good idea to leave the house for 20-30 minutes at a time so that your TT gets used to the sound of you leaving and returning. TTs have incredible sensory perception, and it won't be long before he can anticipate your return before he's even heard a sound. Similarly, when you leave, he will eventually just shrug and get settled in his bed or crate.

66

USE A KENNEL OR CRATE OR BLOCK OFF A SMALL AREA OF YOUR HOME

When leaving the house, most TT owners prefer to leave their dogs in an outdoor kennel or indoor crate. Many owners prefer kennels as they not only keep your TT safe but also your property.

If you are unable to have a kennel and do not want to use a crate for whatever reason, you should leave your TT in a small area of your home, such as a bedroom with the door shut or with a baby gate in the doorway. Or consider a bathroom or kitchen area if it has space.

In time, you can give your TT more freedom in the house when he's alone, although you should wait until he is trustworthy. Many people rush this process, and it can result in your TT developing bad habits when you're not around to supervise him.

 USE PUZZLE-TYPE TOYS SUCH AS KONGS

Make sure your TT has plenty of tempting chew toys to keep him occupied when you leave your home for the first time. Kong rubber toys have cavities you can fill with tasty treats. Your TT has to work to get the food out, which is a game he can enjoy for quite a while after you've left the building. Tibetan Terriers absolutely love solving puzzles.

Here are some tips to make a Kong toy more interesting to your TT:

- Cut back on your TT's meals or feed him in the Kong so that he will be more interested in the toy when he is left alone.

- Stuff the Kong with smelly, tempting food like cooked hamburger or wet dog food or even peanut butter.

- Freeze the Kong overnight so that your TT has to work even harder to get the food out of it. Bear in mind that Kongs are not indestructible, and you will have to replace the toys every now and then.

- Leave a few Kongs if you need to keep your TT entertained for longer. Stuff one with food that is really easy to get out and make the others a little more difficult but with a really tempting aroma.

HELPFUL TIP
The Puppy Shed

When your Tibetan Terrier is a puppy, he'll have a soft coat of fur that he'll entirely shed at some point before he's a year old to make way for his adult coat. The adult coat is made up of a downy undercoat and a silky outer layer. The Tibetan Terrier puppy coat is simple to care for, and it's a great idea to establish a grooming routine with your dog at an early age.

Photo Courtesy of Beth Gillahan

Hiring a Trusted Dog Walker

A trusted helper can be really useful if you don't have time to return from work during the day to check on your pup and give him some exercise and a potty break. Ask a friend or hire a professional dog walker to come by and meet your TT so that both the dog and the sitter become familiar with each other. A sitter doesn't have to stay with your TT the entire time you're away. Even having someone pay a brief visit to your TT while you're gone will ensure you have a little bit of peace of mind, and your new companion will be comforted.

You can find professional dog walkers in your area on platforms like Rover.com or Care.com or by doing a simple internet search.

Consider Doggy Daycare

If you take on a TT when you know you are required to work long hours and he will have to adjust to being alone, doggie daycare can be very useful. Using doggie daycare all the time would be extremely expensive, but once a week can help in the early days of leaving your TT home alone or if you have a particularly long day of work ahead of you.

Using a Camera When Your Tibetan Terrier Is Home Alone

An indoor camera can give you a huge amount of peace of mind when you leave your TT home alone for the first time. With a camera, you'll be connected to your TT throughout the day so that you can check on him at any time. However, cameras don't replace your presence, so you may still want to get someone to check on your TT when you're first away from home. Also, bear in mind that you may well see something on the camera that you

Photo Courtesy
of Julie Boncher

don't want to, such as an escape from a crate and your dog then chewing up something important. This is another very valid reason for following the crate training method laid out in Chapter 6.

Keep Other Pets Separated at First

If your TT is not the only animal sharing your home, it's a good idea to keep him apart while you're out for the first time. This is particularly true if you haven't had sufficient time to let everyone get to know one another.

You can keep your pets crated in their respective areas, or you can physically separate the animals in different rooms with the doors shut. Just make sure that your animals can't gain access to each other while you're out, as they will almost certainly get into mischief!

What About a Doggie Door When Your Tibetan Terrier Is Left Home Alone?

If your TT has access to a safely enclosed backyard via a doggie door, in theory, he is okay as far as potty breaks are concerned. However, TTs can get bored very quickly when you're not around, and so you probably want to think twice about allowing easy access to anywhere the dog can cause carnage, like destroying flower beds or digging underneath the fence.

Once you have gotten to know your TT's personality and comfort level in terms of being left alone all day, you can decide if a doggy door is right for you. Take care with this decision if you have a newly adopted TT, as you don't know for sure if he has Houdini tendencies.

If you do decide to use a doggy door, make sure that you:

- Exercise your TT before you leave and when you come back home so that he is less inclined to bolt through the doggy door as soon as you leave.
- Leave stimulating toys like food puzzles or doggie chews, although not too many, and rotate the ones you have so that your dog doesn't lose interest in them.
- Install cameras for your backyard and place a sign so that potential intruders or dog thieves aren't tempted to break in.
- Avoid using a doggy door if you have toxic plants in your backyard or if there's a possibility of poisonous snakes or spiders.

What Does Your Tibetan Terrier Get Up to When You're Gone?

Once your TT is housebroken, fully grown, and you have developed a great relationship, you can leave him alone for about six hours, although less would definitely be better. If your Tibetan Terrier was leader of the pack, you would probably never be allowed to leave the house again; such is his desire to remain by your side at all times.

Photo Courtesy
of Lorraine Clark

Generally speaking, if your TT has been fed and well-exercised before you leave, he can easily fill those six hours with activities such as:

- Naps
- Gazing out of the window
- Entertaining himself with dog chews and Kong toys
- Tuning in to the sounds of the outside world

After those six hours, at the very least, your TT will need a potty break. Better yet, a walk and/or some playtime with his favorite human will make being on his own more than worth the while!

Other tips for when you leave your TT alone:

- Remain calm yourself when it's time to go. If you are anxious, your TT will sense it and become anxious too.

- Leave on a radio or TV for music or background noise, as it will comfort your TT.

- Stick rigidly to a routine, leaving your TT in the same place every time you leave home.

- Don't say goodbye to your TT. Just leave in silence without even making eye contact. If you make a big hoo-hah of leaving, he'll get upset.

- Don't expect too much from your TT on the first occasion he's home alone. It takes time for dogs to adjust to new routines and strange environments, so give him plenty of slack. The adjustment could take a few weeks, so remain patient.

- If your TT shows anxiety when you leave by crying or whining, don't assume he has separation anxiety. Although Tibetan Terriers have a propensity for this behavior, he is almost certainly just a little anxious that he's being left alone for the first time. Ignore the whining, and he will very quickly adjust. (For more about separation anxiety, see Chapter 9.)

CHAPTER 8

The Importance of Socialization

Properly Socializing Your Puppy

> *Make sure to socialize your TT, starting as a puppy and continuing into adulthood. Too much time spent at home makes TTs wary of travel or outings. Make sure to get them out on a leash, meeting other dogs and people. The more socialization they have as a puppy they better adaptable they are with traveling as an adult. Here's a tip: bring their favorite blanket, bed or toy with you. They like to have some of their security from home with them when they are away.*
>
> RENE' STAMM
> *Euphoria Tibetans*

Your most important job is to help your TT become a well-adjusted puppy. Here are some tips to help you.

1 Don't put off socializing your puppy because the sooner you can start, the easier it will be for your TT to develop his social skills.

2 Be aware of your TT pup's body language, and if he looks stressed, help him out. Be prepared to take prompt action if your TT has a negative experience when you first start to socialize him.

3 Find a local puppy class and sign up as soon as you can. That way, both you and your TT pup can socialize together and have a good time.

Photo Courtesy of Clare Beale

TT pups who don't get lots of opportunities to interact positively with other dogs, new people, or novel situations and environments can often become nervous and withdrawn or even aggressive.

Although your TT is able to learn new tricks at any age, young puppies have a particular sweet spot between the ages of 13 and 14 weeks when they are particularly receptive to learning new skills. During this critical time, your TT is building his impression of the world and what is normal and acceptable in it. At this time, more than any other in your TT's life, if he has lots of social stimuli that give him positive experiences interacting with others, he will have a solid foundation for the future.

Most TT owners know about the importance of socializing their pups. However, you have to be careful about how you go about it so that your TT isn't exposed to negative experiences that emphasize the dangers in the world rather than its delights.

As with all aspects of your TT's training, it's all about balance. Here are some steps you can take to introduce your TT to the world in a way that will broaden his horizons and build his confidence.

How to keep your TT pup's experiences positive when socializing him:

- Socialization isn't just about introducing your puppy to new things but also about ensuring these experiences are positive ones. You should monitor all interactions carefully and observe your pup's body language to make sure he is not overwhelmed or afraid of the new situation. Try to resist picking him up to remove him from a situation unless he is in danger, but at all times, be ready to protect your TT if he displays signs of anxiety, stress, or fear. Imagine your first day at kindergarten and how big and intimidating everything seemed. Magnify that a little, and that's what your TT is feeling when he first begins to socialize.

> **FUN FACT**
> **Tibetan Terriers at Downton Abbey**
>
> Actor Hugh Bonneville, best known for his role as Lord Grantham on the hit historical drama Downton Abbey, is the proud owner of a pair of Tibetan Terriers. Bonneville's dogs are named Sasha and Teddy, and they make their home in West Sussex. "They demand a lot of tummy scratching and, in the evenings, they just want to be pampered," Bonneville said in an interview with Country Life in 2019.

- When you first start to socialize your TT, try and keep encounters relatively brief while he gets used to different situations. If you take your pup to your child's soccer game, for example, there's a chance you could be distracted, and your TT might become the center of attention for kids wanting to pet the cute puppy unsupervised. Take short trips to events with the intention of staying no more than half an hour until your TT is completely relaxed in that particular environment.

- Lots of frequent, short socialization sessions are particularly good for young TT pups. Rather than going out, invite friends of different ages, genders, and ethnicities to your home for no longer than 10 minutes to meet your new pup. That way, your TT will be exposed to a good variety of new and interesting people but not for so long that it can all go horribly wrong. It's impossible to predict who your TT pup will take a shine to and who he won't, although you should always keep in mind a Tibetan Terrier's tendency to be a little standoffish with people he's not sure of.

- Make sure you monitor all the humans and other animals in your socialization situations, especially if your TT is unfamiliar with dogs. Being handled in the wrong way can make your TT pup feel unstable and unsafe, so you need to be involved in every interaction.

Expose Your Pup to New People at Home

Your home is very often the one place that's ignored when it comes to socializing new TT pups. Many owners prefer to take their dogs to public places with lots of people to get them used to the outside world. However, the best way for your TT to meet human beings is on his own territory, as it will give him more confidence with new encounters.

Socializing your TT at home doesn't just apply to other people and children—invite some doggy guests too. It's great to get your TT used to having other dogs on his property because if you can achieve that, all other socialization will be much easier. TTs are extremely territorial, mostly because they are possessive about their humans, making socialization a really good way of teaching them to chill out in the company of others.

Socializing at Puppy Kindergarten

"

A beginner puppy class will create a bond with your new puppy. Tibetans are very smart, and don't need the same exercise repeated more than 2 or 3 times. When your training session is over, take a break from classes. Go back to an advanced beginner or intermediate level class when your puppy is a year or two old, and you will be amazed at how much they remember.

JACKIE FAUST
Arkeden Tibetan Terriers

"

TT pups from as young as eight weeks old can meet other dogs and people in a controlled environment like puppy kindergarten classes. Reputable classes will require your TT pup to have had at least one vaccine and will also disinfect classroom spaces between groups of puppies to reduce the risk of communicable diseases. Take time to find the right puppy classes for your treasured TT so that he has a safe environment that builds his confidence.

Before you put down your cash and sign up for a puppy class, observe a session without your puppy. Take time to observe how the instructors manage the session. Are they mindful of Tibetan Terrier-specific playing styles? You want to know that your TT pup will be mixed with breeds of a similar size and temperament rather than paired with a German Shepherd, for example, which would almost certainly be too boisterous for your more delicate pupster. Watch how the instructors intervene and redirect the behavior of dogs that could easily escalate into an unpleasant situation.

Most of all, puppy classes should have a no-holds-barred area for canine infants. Like human kindergartens, play is one of the best ways to socialize our furry counterparts so that they learn self-control and respect for others.

But it won't all be about play at puppy kindergarten because socialization is important in all settings. You want your TT to be able to sit calmly next to another dog without automatically engaging in frenzied play. So don't be tempted to think that because your TT isn't exhausted after a class that he hasn't learned something valuable.

With any puppy classes, it is vital that your TT is able to avoid inappropriate four-legged friends who could potentially teach him bad habits. While play is really important for your TT pup, you don't want him to start morphing into the school bully! Despite his relatively diminutive size, a Tibetan Terrier still has the capacity to become way too big for his boots!

One of the worst habits your TT pup can learn through play is being too rough or having no impulse control. If he is allowed to play in an aggressive

Photo Courtesy
of Christine Hadley

way, it will be easy for your TT to learn those negative behaviors. Once a dog has practiced bad behaviors, it can be extremely difficult to correct him further down the line.

A big lesson your TT can learn at puppy kindergarten is that being calm has tangible benefits. Your TT should be able to go to the instructor when called and focus on him completely before being allowed to return to play. That will teach the dog that it pays to be polite to others!

Good puppy classes will provide your TT puppy with a blend of play and training, perhaps with a little grooming mixed in to give him the experience of being handled. Everything he learns should give him the confidence he needs to feel secure in the world around him.

When Puppies Meet Adult Dogs

> *I always pick up a puppy when meeting new people or dogs so it is not frightened by the experience. Don't expect it to defend itself from another dog, you need to protect it.*
>
> TANE KLEIST
> *Kildare Tibetan Terriers*

Although playing with other puppies will be really stimulating for your TT, it is also a good idea to organize positive interactions with older dogs. Older dogs that are well-trained provide a great example to puppy counterparts, and they will intuitively be aware that your TT is still a baby that requires gentle but playful handling. Older dogs also know when they are required to play the part of tutors to young charges.

Make sure you screen any older dogs you invite to play with your TT. Some owners are completely unaware that their dogs lack social graces or don't like other animals. Remember that although you think your TT is the most adorable pup in the world, his cuteness is not going to miraculously change an older dog's behavior.

Ask how the potential playmate is around other dogs and find out what you can about his playing style. Tibetan Terriers love chasing things and exploring the environment. If you have a shy TT who has a playmate who is more into rough-housing, your TT is not likely to want to play.

What Vets Say About Puppy Socialization

It's hard to believe, but one of the biggest obstacles to socializing your puppy is your vet! Although no vet wants to see a puppy develop into a growling hermit, a vet's focus is entirely on ensuring your TT isn't exposed to any communicable diseases (fair enough). For this reason, most vets will advise you not to take your TT pup out into the world until he has had his last vaccine and is fully immunized, which is typically at 16 weeks.

Although it is understandable why many vets are cautious in this respect, this mentality can unwittingly create an extremely difficult situation. The number one reason dogs of all breeds are surrendered to shelters is behavioral problems. If your TT pup isn't socialized properly from a very young age, he can develop separation anxiety, which is very difficult to overcome. From a TT owner's perspective, the odds of your pup developing a behavioral problem are more serious than the prospect of parvovirus or kennel cough.

Photo Courtesy of Neil Ravey

There are recent studies that have concluded that puppies with one vaccination were at no greater risk of contracting parvovirus at socialization classes than vaccinated puppies who did not attend at all. Naturally, much depends on the puppy class following good sanitary protocols.

It is worth noting the following statement by the American Veterinary Society of Animal Behavior on the subject of socialization:

During [the first 3 months of life] puppies should be exposed to as many new people, animals, stimuli and environments as can be achieved safely and without causing overstimulation manifested as excessive fear, withdrawal or avoidance behavior. For this reason, the American Veterinary Society of Animal Behavior believes that it should be the standard of care for puppies to receive such socialization before he is fully vaccinated.

Even though the attitude towards socialization has changed, you may find that your vet is still not open to the idea. Ultimately, however, your TT pup is YOUR responsibility, and you can safely socialize your pride and joy before full immunization in these ways:

- Invite friends and family over to your home. Mix it up with children, adults, men, women, the Amazon delivery driver, the gardeners, and anyone else you can drag into your home to vary how your TT pup sees and experiences a wide variety of people.
- Take your puppy to a friend's house. Just entering a new environment will offer your TT lots of new and engaging experiences.
- Invite anyone with a healthy, vaccinated, and puppy-friendly dog over for a playdate. Playing with other dogs makes a big difference to your TT's social development, and he will learn important things like how to share and play without biting.
- Take your TT pup for a short walk somewhere there is no danger of feces or urine from other animals. An empty parking lot is often a convenient place for this kind of adventure.
- Go to the park and take a blanket with you. Set down the blanket for you and your TT to snuggle up together where you can people and dog watch from your safe place.
- Take your TT for a ride in your car. Help him get used to traveling with you by just taking a short ride around the block or to the store and back. Just don't leave your pup in the car alone.
- Visit cafés that have terrace or sidewalk seating. Set your TT pup down on a mat, which you can take with you, and let him observe what's going on around him. TTs have huge supplies of curiosity, which often borders on nosiness!

Expose Your Pup to a Variety of Things

> *Young puppies need to be taken on 'sniff walks' where they dictate how much running and stopping and sniffing they do. Taking a five or six month puppy to run with you 2 miles a day is a really, really bad idea. Puppies joints tendons and ligaments take a long time to grow and you don't want to much stress on them until they're 18 months to two years old.*
>
> MAUREEN DWYER
> *Yonpo Tibetan Terriers*

Socializing your TT pup isn't just about exposing him to new people and places; it's also about getting him used to a variety of experiences. There are all sorts of things your pup needs to get used to—loud noises like ambulances and vacuum cleaners; people that move oddly, such as toddlers or someone on crutches; different surfaces like cattle grids or manhole covers; and all types of weather.

Photo Courtesy of Paula Boyd

You should make sure your TT pup is introduced to modern conveniences like elevators and automatic doors. Of course, if you live in a rural setting, there is less need to focus on this aspect of socialization. If this is the case, think about the noises your TT will be exposed to where you live, such as heavy machinery and various animal and bird noises for a start. Wherever your home is, view it from your TT's eyes and consider everything that could be potentially frightening to him. That way, you can use treats and positive reinforcement to remove his fears.

Never Force a Scared Tibetan Terrier Puppy

> *We tell our new families that they are their dog's BEST advocate, so if it's in the vet's office, or on the sidewalk in town, and you're feeling uncomfortable, pick that puppy up. It's your job, we tell them, to keep that puppy safe until they're older when they can absorb stressful things more easily.*
>
> MAUREEN DWYER
> *Yonpo Tibetan Terriers*

Tibetan Terriers have extremely sensitive souls, and your dog will inevitably encounter a situation that he will find frightening. The answer is to not make him "deal with it" but instead give him the space to come to terms with his fear in his own time.

Say, for example, your TT pup reacts nervously to a man wearing a hat. Don't be tempted to place your TT in the man's lap, hoping that the dog will get over his fear quickly. Your TT will want to be at your side when he is introduced to this strange being, and if the man takes a seat and happens to have juicy treats, your pup will be quick to warm to him.

Some trainers advocate ignoring fearful behavior in puppies, but this simply doesn't work with Tibetan Terriers. They become very anxious if you don't acknowledge when they are communicating fear to you. If you allow your TT to remain in a situation that makes him fearful, it can cause long-term damage to his mental health. Your dog will also lose trust in you and may even become depressed.

Places NOT to Take Your New Pup

Although socialization is vital, it is also important to avoid places where there's any risk of endangering your TT pup's health or safety. You also want to avoid giving your TT a negative association with the world around him.

Here are some of the places you should NOT consider for socializing your pup until he is fully vaccinated:

- Off-leash dog parks
- Anywhere there could be stray dogs or accumulation of feces
- Somewhere there's a possibility of encountering sick dogs
- Any establishments where he could encounter drunk and rowdy humans
- Anywhere he has to be left unattended or in a hot car. NEVER tie up your puppy outside the grocery store!
- Any event that your TT might find uncomfortable, such as a Little League game or a Fourth of July fireworks display
- Anywhere you won't be able to devote your complete attention to your TT pup to make him feel safe and secure.

Socializing an Adult Adopted or Rescue Tibetan Terrier

If you are bringing a TT home of any age, you will need to socialize him to his new environment and all its sights and sounds. Say your TT was rescued from a rural area, and you're bringing him home to a cityscape. You'll need to get him used to all the sounds from passing trucks and motorcycles.

Conversely, if your TT has been a city dog and you live in the country, you'll need to socialize your TT to the sound of the neighboring farm animals or coyotes during the night.

Even if a shelter is unable to tell you very much about your TT's past, his body language in different settings can give you very good clues as to how he is feeling.

If your TT has experienced negative situations in his past, it could well have been during the most critical time of his development as a puppy, between 3 and 16 weeks. That will make it more likely for him to be fearful of new things.

Reading your Tibetan Terrier's Body Language

You can learn a great deal by observing your TT's body language. The best way of socializing a rescue TT to any unfamiliar sights, sounds, and experiences is to let him take things at his own pace.

When out socializing your rescue or adopted TT, look for the following signs of discomfort, anxiety, or fear in his body language:

- Tail tucked under
- Flattened ears
- Lip or nose licking (typically multiple times)
- Yawning
- Shaking
- Crouching down
- Attempting to run away or hide
- Whining
- Hair standing on end on the neck or spine, known as piloerection

If you push your TT into a situation where he is uncomfortable, he can feel overwhelmed and shut down. Dogs will literally sink to the ground or cling to your legs. Being in this state is so distressing for a Tibetan Terrier that he can easily form negative associations, which are very difficult to alter.

Rather than using this approach, it is much better to take things at your new buddy's pace so that he is able to adjust to new people, environments, and situations without any pressure. You take on a big responsibility with a rescue or adopted TT, most often in restoring his faith in humankind. Even if your TT's issues seem insurmountable, patience and consistency will bring him out of his shell, and the rewards are absolutely priceless.

The Role of Negative Past Experiences

In many cases, rescued or adopted TTs have had negative past experiences. If a TT feels the need to constantly defend himself because of these experiences, it can manifest as aggression. If you learn the language of a TT's defensive behavior, you can diffuse situations before they get out of hand. Here is the body language your TT might display if he feels threatened:

- Barking
- Lunging

- Snarling
- Growling
- Baring teeth

If you notice any of these signs, you might want to consider combining your socialization efforts with help from a certified professional dog trainer. If a dog has deep-rooted behavioral issues, you'll need professional help.

Photo Courtesy of Alexandra Marckx

Best Practices to Socialize a Rescue or Adopted Adult Tibetan Terrier

Not all rescue or adopted TTs will become defensive when around other dogs, people, busy streets, etc. Rather, your dog might just be hesitant. You can use the following tips to gradually introduce him to his new surroundings in a positive way.

1 Keep encounters positive: Remember, TTs of all ages love nothing more than praise, so you should heap it on him while out socializing. If you're introducing your TT to other dogs, it may be better not to use treats to reward him as it could result in a squabble with his potential furry friends. Reward your TT if he makes small advances, such as looking at the thing he's scared of and not reacting to it. Don't force your TT to interact with anything or anyone until he is absolutely ready.

2 Keep encounters brief: If you're introducing your TT to other dogs while on-leash, you can get a good idea if the other dog is friendly. If the dogs have a good initial reaction to each other, you can let your TT have a good sniff before praising him and moving on swiftly. The longer you hang around, the more likely that either your TT or the other dog will become uncomfortable.

3 Start with less challenging environments or encounters: you ideally want to keep your TT within his stress threshold. If he is relaxed, he will be much more susceptible to learning. However, once stress kicks in, all learning goes flying out of the window. Your TT has to be in the right state of mind for socialization. If your goal is to navigate a busy street, start off with a quiet residential area until your dog has the confidence to take the next step. Slowly build up the amount of activity surrounding your TT while you walk so that, eventually, he is able to cope seamlessly with the hustle and bustle.

CHAPTER 9

Early Training for a Well-Behaved Tibetan Terrier

Establishing Your Leadership

As with our kids, it's important that you are your TT's leader and not his best friend. Your TT pup will be looking to you to be his "parent" and provide him with everything he needs. That includes a safe environment that has structure and stability so that he feels secure and confident.

From the outset, you need to start developing your role as leader so that your pup takes cues from you to understand what he can and can't do. This will help him understand the ground rules of your home and also how to behave when he is out in public.

The key elements of successful TT leadership are consistency and patience, and you should also bear in mind that your pup may get up to some antics! Tibetan Terriers are particularly curious by nature, and your new pup will be intent on figuring things out, so be prepared for some mishaps along the way.

Once your role as leader has been accepted by your TT, you will both go on to develop a lifelong bond of trust and love. Once your relationship has become more established through training, you'll find your TT will become your closest companion and a well-behaved member of the family too.

There are a few ways you can establish yourself as your TT's pack leader that don't involve basic obedience commands:

Get Him to Work for His Food

Although I'm not suggesting your TT needs to get a job to pay for his own kibble, feeding time can be an excellent training opportunity for pups. If you are feeding your pup three times a day, try using one session to work on some commands.

For an extra challenge you can ask your pup to "sit" and wait while you set his food bowl down. Mark correct behavior by simply saying "good," and then allow him to eat the rest of his meal. The incentive of a bowl of smelly food works great as part of your pup's training regime.

Photo Courtesy of Linda Middlemiss

Don't Let Your Puppy Graze

Photo Courtesy
of Caron Kay

It's really important that you train your pup to finish his food in one sitting. Many owners leave a half-eaten bowl of food so their dogs can graze whenever they want to. The main reason this is a bad idea is that your TT likes to know when he is going to eat. If he has access to food the entire day, he will be more likely to ignore it.

By removing the food bowl if he is not finished after 5 or 10 minutes of being out, your TT pup will learn that his food is set out at certain times for a certain duration and will eat within this "window" you have created.

Keep Him in His Crate During Your Dinnertime

Tibetan Terriers can be extremely sneaky and opportunistic. There's nothing more enticing than tasty food that falls from your dinner table. If your pup is allowed to roam the house while you eat, there's a good chance you'll find him gazing up at you, eagerly awaiting scraps from your table.

You can show your puppy what you'd like him to do while you eat by placing him in his crate or a playpen when you're going to sit down to eat dinner. Give your puppy a chew toy to play with, or simply let him relax and make it one of his designated nap times. This will educate him on how to behave during mealtimes and prevent any begging at the table!

Who is Leading Who on the Leash?

Establishing your leadership is particularly important when it comes to taking your TT pup on his first walk. You can start working on this before you even leave the house for the first time. Your TT's natural curiosity will make him want to race through any door as soon as it opens. This can be potentially dangerous, and so it's a good idea to get him used to waiting at thresholds before crossing. This training can prevent impulsive behavior in your pup and make leash training much easier.

You can use this training to control your TT's urge to dart, asking him to sit before you put on a leash and pausing before going out of the door. You don't have to go any further than your doorstep, but when you're exiting, make sure you are either stepping out together or with you in the lead. Never let your TT get ahead of you on the leash, as he will consider himself in charge.

As you progress to walking your pup outdoors, at first, he may not want to walk where you want to take him, and he'll probably be all over the place. That is completely normal, although it's your job as his leader to help reduce any leash-pulling, teaching him to follow your lead when outside instead of his own instincts.

Your home really is the best place to start introducing your pup to walking on a leash. You can walk him from one room to another or around the backyard or driveway and slowly extend the radius from there. In the early days of walking your TT pup, he should have "working walks" lasting between 15 and 30 minutes, including combined walking and command practice.

A dog that darts through every open door can be problematic. That's why it is highly recommended to practice control at thresholds so that you eliminate the possibility of your TT running into a busy road or pulling you over as he runs off in pursuit of something.

The Right Way to Play with Your Tibetan Terrier Pup

"

Tibetans are very intelligent and are very easy to train. You typically only have to show them something once or twice and they know how to do it. On the down side of that, if you accidentally show them something you don't want them to know how to do, it's already too late. They already know how to do it and won't forget!

NIKKIE KINZIGER
Ri Lee Kennels

"

Photo Courtesy of Glynis Carroll

Playtime is another great opportunity to establish yourself as your TT's leader. Although everyone will want to play with your adorable pup, it is still important to make sure that you are showing him desirable behavior.

For example, if you're playing tug-of-war with your TT, use the "drop it" command to get him to let go of his end of the rope. This gives you an opportunity to lead playtime while managing your TT's energy levels at the same time.

The benefit of structured playtime is that it helps your pup learn good manners while having fun. It sets boundaries as to what's acceptable and what isn't. As the leader of playtime, you can start and stop games when you want and use the drop it command to get your pup to release his toy when you feel he needs a break.

The drop it command is actually very useful in other situations where you need to take back something your pup has that he shouldn't, like one of your best shoes. Through play, he'll have learned to associate the command with releasing the item, which he should do so straight away.

Help Your Tibetan Terrier Get Used to Being Handled

It's a great idea to get your pup used to being touched in different areas of his body. For one thing, your TT has a high-maintenance coat and will need regular grooming when he's fully grown, and you don't want him to be nervous about the experience. You'll also want to confidently introduce him to other people of all ages, as well as your groomer, and so it makes sense to get him used to being touched before these encounters.

Obviously, when the dog is little, you don't have to pass him around for all and sundry to cuddle him, but you should introduce handling into your one-to-one training. Including grooming and handling in his daily routine will also help to strengthen your bond and build more trust between you and him as his leader.

When introducing a new brush, grooming glove, or hairdryer, make it a comfortable experience by using your TT's food as a reward while slowly showing him the new item. It might take a while for your TT to feel comfortable around grooming tools, but it's worth being persistent and making a few attempts at it.

This teaches your TT to be fine with handling and grooming and also is a method of early socialization. You are your TT's leader, and so it's up to you to find opportunities to safely expose him to real-life situations that will help him become a well-adjusted adult.

Photo Courtesy
of Kimberley Laidler

Set the Tone for Greeting Guests

TTs of all ages can become very excitable when someone new arrives at the house, and you have to make sure you guide your dog in the correct way to behave. It's a good idea to keep him in a separate area when someone arrives at your home. This will give him enough time to settle down while he's aware of someone new being in his home.

Although it's important to teach your pup to greet guests the correct way, humans also need education on how to greet him! People have an

HELPFUL TIP
Do TTs Bark a Lot?

Watchdog tendencies run deep with Tibetan Terriers, and it's not uncommon for this breed to bark when they see or hear something out of the ordinary. However, if your Tibetan Terrier is barking excessively, it may be due to boredom, loneliness, or attention-seeking behavior. Addressing the root cause of the barking is the first step to mitigate this unwanted behavior. Next, use positive reinforcement to reward your dog when he's quiet.

impulsive reaction when they see an adorable TT puppy, and the temptation to gush over him can be hard to resist. Ask your visitors to keep their emotions in check. Ask them not to give your TT any attention at all if he is jumping up or barking. Only when he has settled down and his energy levels have dropped should your guests reward your dog with his attention. For a Tibetan Terrier, attention is the ultimate goal and better than an edible treat any day of the week!

Greeting guests in a composed manner is another daily occurrence you need to prep your dog for. A teeny-weeny TT pup jumping up on people versus a fully grown 24-pounder is quite a different scenario. It's important to respect the fact that not everyone is comfortable around dogs of any breed, and your dog's behavior matters when meeting new people.

Crate Your Puppy to Create Good Habits

We covered crate training in Chapter 6, and now we're going to take a closer look at the benefits of using one as a tool for training your TT pup. Although the temptation to cuddle up to him at night will be strong, you should resist it for your TT's benefit. A crate will make him feel secure while he's developing confidence and independence and will also prevent him from getting into trouble when you're not around to supervise!

Photo Courtesy
of Juan Boria and Michael John

You can use the crate during the daytime to help you introduce structure to your TT's daily routine. Use it as a place for your TT to relax and take some time out from play to get him used to associating the crate with downtime. This will also help your TT get the sleep and naptime he needs.

There are some practical benefits to crate training your TT, such as travel or overnight vet visits. Remember that you are preparing him for day-to-day experiences so that he doesn't struggle to adjust later when he's older.

Although it can be tough to crate train your pup at first, consistently introducing him to it as part of his daily routine will quickly allow him to be comfortable in the space. It's really worth making the effort, too, as it is an asset to have your TT crate trained, particularly as it helps prevent separation anxiety.

Introducing the crate to your TT at an early age will help establish you in a healthy leadership role with him. With every passing day, your bond will grow stronger as he learns to trust the routine you have introduced him to. You'll also have built the foundations of strong communication, which will help your TT thrive and develop into a well-behaved dog.

CHAPTER 10

Housetraining the Easy Way

> "
>
> *Be consistent! If your puppy has an accident, remember it is exactly that... an accident. Your puppy is trying to please you. Accidents in the house fall back on the owner, not the puppy. It is not helpful to scold a puppy that has already gone, instead make sure you praise and reward the times they potty outside.*
>
> RENE' STAMM
> *Euphoria Tibetans*
>
> "

One of the most important steps you can take for a happy life with your TT is to learn how to train your TT pup to use the potty at the right time and place. Research shows that soiling the house is one of the top reasons dogs are rejected from homes or end up in shelters. There are few people who are willing or able to deal with a dog that destroys flooring by constantly leaving a smelly mess for you to clean up.

It is vital that you remember that you are completely responsible for your TT's behavior. In this chapter, we'll take a closer look at the most effective ways to housetrain your TT.

There are three prevailing housetraining methods you can use with your pup, including:

- Crate training
- Paper training
- Frequent walks outside

*Photo Courtesy
of Judy and Mark Price
Taken by Jennifer Linton*

Each method has its pros and cons, although your dog can be successful using any method if you take care to incorporate the following:

- Diet controls

- A regular schedule for feeding and exercise

- Positive reinforcement

Using a Crate as a Potty-Training Tool

As mentioned in Chapter 6, some new TT owners are uncomfortable with the idea of confining a pup to a crate. However, this reluctance soon disappears when it becomes clear that the dog loves the security of his crate. You'll also realize how useful it is for you to know exactly where he is and what he's up to! Remember that your TT likes small spaces to curl up and sleep in, and even if you don't have a crate, he will seek out a suitable spot in your house on his own.

The theory behind using a crate for housetraining is that all dogs prefer to keep their sleeping areas clean. For this reason, you want to make sure your pup's crate isn't so big that he can eliminate in a corner and still find a place to sleep away from his mess. Choose a crate that is just big enough for your pup to lie down, stand up, and turn around. Some larger

Photo Courtesy
of Kelli Murphy

crates have partitions so that you can increase the space available to your pup as he grows.

You'll know when your TT pup wants to use the toilet as he will alert you by whining and scratching. This is his signal that he feels an urge to eliminate and needs to exit his crate. It's really important that you respond to these signals immediately because if he accidentally goes in his crate, your dog will get the idea that it is acceptable behavior. Then the likelihood of finding messes all-around your home is also dramatically increased!

Puppy Pads and Paper Training

In an ideal world, you want your pup to learn to control himself inside your home and only eliminate in designated areas outdoors. However, depending on your circumstances, you might need to get creative. Some people might have jobs that prevent them from popping home to check on a pup during the day. Others live in locations that experience particularly brutal winters, where the opportunity to leave home at all is minimized. It's important that you adapt any training techniques to your specific circumstances.

Puppy pads are a convenient house-training solution that allows you to train your TT to relieve himself in an approved spot inside your home. As your TT matures, you can then shift potty training outdoors so that he learns to eliminate in the same place every time he goes.

Create a Housetraining Schedule for Your Pup

Bear in mind that your TT pup has a teeny-tiny bladder, and it can often seem as though water goes right through him. The same is also true for "number twos." Make sure you give him plenty of opportunities to do the right thing at the right time. Until your pup is a year old, he should be able to control his bladder for the same number of hours as his age in months. That said, every TT pup is different, and there could be a little difference in the timing for each.

Monitor the day's events so that you can create your pup's potty schedule based on his personal habits. With very young pups, you should take them out to potty:

- First thing in the morning
- Before bedtime
- After playing inside
- After spending time alone
- After drinking water

What you have to prepare yourself for is that a young TT will want to use the toilet constantly. This can often mean that you seem to spend your life running into your backyard or to the street, but keep in mind, this is NOT a permanent situation!

The quicker you establish an approved area for elimination and make clear those places in your home that are strictly off-limits, the sooner you'll find everything falls into place quickly for your TT. He is incredibly intelligent and will learn to associate routines with required behaviors very rapidly, so don't give up!

Observe and Supervise at All Times

> 66
>
> *Be consistent. Their little bladders are not that big so they need to eliminate a lot. You can't take them out too often as a puppy. Go to the same area in your yard and choose a word or a phrase such as 'go potty' or 'get busy' so they do their job. Do not play with them until they do what they are expected to do. Then it's high praise!*
>
> NIKKIE KINZIGER
> *Ri Lee Kennels*
>
> 99

As you get to know your TT, you'll recognize individual signals that he is going to eliminate. Some pups will have to go potty every time they play or get excited, whereas others will develop an ability to control themselves for longer. Just the same as with babies, your TT's potty habits are completely individual to him.

Control His Diet

A puppy has an immature digestive system, and so he really can't handle too much food. Break up his feeding schedule into three small daily meals for the early days and weeks of his life. You should also ensure you give your TT the best-quality puppy food you can afford.

Many vets and pet retail outlets carry different brands of "nutritional platforms." Each has a different formula to meet the specific needs of particular canine breeds, including Tibetan Terriers. You should look out for dry food formulas that contain real meat as a principal ingredient and do not have any added colors or flavorings.

It sounds unpleasant, but examining your TT's poop is the best way for you to figure out if anything in his diet is causing issues. If he is consistently eliminating stools that are loose and smelly, he might need a change in diet. Similarly, if he is constipated, there will almost certainly be a dietary reason. It's a good idea to consult your vet in the early days of your TT's life to ensure he is getting the best nutritional value for his food.

Use Plenty of Positive Reinforcement

"

Pay lots of attention to where the puppy is for the first two or three weeks, you can attach them to you with a long leash and perhaps crate them when you're not able to pay attention to them. It's nice when you're able to establish errorless learning for potty training right away. Also if there are accidents in the house, NO punishment should be used, they are babies still and it's generally our fault when accidents happen.

MAUREEN DWYER
Yonpo Tibetan Terriers

"

Unless you catch him in the actual act of soiling on your best rug, there is absolutely no point in scolding your TT. He has a very short memory. If you castigate him for destroying your shoes before you came home from work, your dog will be completely confused as to why you're upset, having already forgotten he chewed something.

Remember that your TT is not being intentionally naughty. He is learning a valuable life lesson with house-

FUN FACT
Tibetan Terrier Association (TTA)

The Tibetan Terrier Association (TTA) was founded in 1967 and was recognized by the UK Kennel Club in the same year. Membership in this association includes a subscription to the quarterly club magazine, *TT Talk*. The TTA operates in the United Kingdom and promotes the health and integrity of the breed through education, shows, and rescue efforts.

training, and as with everything else you need to teach him, patience and consistency are key.

Some people think that rubbing a dog's nose in his poop is the best way of teaching him not to mess in the wrong place again. However, if you do this, your TT will very quickly learn to fear you, which will damage your relationship. It also won't teach him not to potty in the house.

The best way of house-training your TT is through positive reinforcement. Tibetan Terriers of all ages are people-pleasers. They will do almost anything for your approval.

If your TT has an accident—and he almost certainly will—don't make a fuss. Don't even acknowledge the mess and just quickly clean it up, using a good product that kills odors. You ideally want to remove the scent so that your dog is not tempted to eliminate at the same place again. As mentioned above, telling him off after the fact will only serve to confuse him and make him fearful of you.

If you see your pup preparing to eliminate by squatting or walking around in circles, pick him up immediately and take him to the designated spot. If he then does the job outside, give him lots of praise and attention, and he'll learn to associate going potty correctly with the pleasure of having your complete focus on him.

Photo Courtesy
of Vivian Hawkins

Housetraining Problems

No matter how experienced with dogs you are, there will almost certainly be times when things don't go to plan. Although we've identified some tips to make housetraining easier, if you are still having problems after a few weeks, it could be that your TT has some physical or behavioral issue that requires further investigation. You should take him to a vet for a complete workup to ensure he is healthy, and if he is, consider finding a trainer or behavioral therapist with experience dealing with this issue.

Here are some common complaints that trainers say they have encountered from TT owners:

"MY TT PUP IS MESSING ALL OVER MY HOME!"

This can often happen when a crate isn't used for housetraining and shows why it is so important to designate one place for toilet use. Once your TT has eliminated in the wrong place in your home, it can be extremely difficult to completely remove his scent. TTs have an incredibly powerful sense of smell that is much better than your own. You'll need to make sure you use an enzymatic cleaner for pet stains. Being consistent in your training can prevent this problem from developing, and as mentioned, make sure to give heaps of praise when your dog does the right thing.

"I GAVE HIM THE RUN OF MY HOME. WHEN I RETURNED, THERE WAS A MESS."

Giving a dog of any age too much space when he is adjusting to a new environment is a big mistake, albeit very common. Introducing him to your daily schedule slowly in the early days will get him used to your routine, but until he is very familiar with behavior expectations, you should ensure he is contained when you're not around. In all honesty, the phrase "curiosity killed the cat" is applicable to Tibetan Terriers!

"HE'S SOILING HIS CRATE!"

If you got your TT from a pet store, shelter, or foster home where he may have been confined for long periods of time, this could be a problem. Your dog may have learned that there is no alternative but to mess in his crate due to the lack of options available to him. This is not a behavioral problem, however, and can be easily addressed by following these steps:

- Observe your TT and assess how well he can control his bladder and bowels when he's not in his crate.

- Take a look at his diet and exercise schedule. Do they need adjusting?

Photo Courtesy
of Linda Middlemiss

- Take your dog for frequent trips outside: first thing in the morning, after every meal, and the last thing at night. If you feel he needs to go more frequently, let him set that pace.

- If you work or are away from home for several hours a day, consider hiring a dog walker to drop by so your TT can relieve himself.

- Thoroughly clean everything with the right product to eliminate any odors left behind if your dog should potty in the wrong place.

How Long Does Puppy Housetraining Take?

There is no hard-and-fast rule as to how long it takes to housetrain your TT. There are all sorts of factors to consider, such as his age, learning history, the training methods you use, and whether you are consistent. You should see progress as your pup matures and a visible difference in his manners from when you first brought him home.

How long it takes to housetrain a Tibetan Terrier can vary wildly from dog to dog. That said, a healthy TT that has received consistent training should have good manners by the time he is five months old. If not, there could be an underlying reason you'll need professional help to identify.

CHAPTER 11
Daily Life with Your Tibetan Terrier

> TTs do not require a lot of exercise as adults. Puppies however do need controlled playtime to help expel their energy. Some sessions of fetch, setting up some basic agility equipment in your yard, and short walks help your puppy get the exercise they need. If you want to take your TT on long walks, runs or more demanding outings this is something you must work up to. Mental stimulation is just as important as physical exercise. Snuggle mats and treat puzzles are a great way to stimulate their mind.
>
> RENE' STAMM
> *Euphoria Tibetans*

There is more to consider about the practicalities of dog ownership if you aren't sharing a household with others. That said, the bond that can form between a TT and his lone parent can be every bit as strong and enduring as his bond with an entire family, sometimes even more so. In this chapter, we focus on how to prepare for life with your TT if you're on your own so that you both get maximum fulfillment from your relationship.

Perhaps because of his ancestral history as a herdsman's companion, a TT is somewhat better equipped to live with a single person than other canine breeds. Although a TT very much enjoys a family environment, he can very quickly become an integral part of a single person's life. One of your main responsibilities, if you are considering adopting or buying a TT, is to ensure you are able to provide the right care for him on your own.

Here are some tips to help you:

Be Ready to Feed Him

Before he even arrives at your home, you'll need to make sure you get the right food for your dog. You can't afford to be impulsive when you decide to take a TT home and should have the most basic supplies in place for his arrival. Buy his dog food, food, and water bowls, and have them waiting in the spot you want him to eat and drink at when he first walks through the door.

Plan-out Vet Visits

Taking your TT anywhere is a little harder when you have to do it alone, despite his relatively small size. It's not always easy to take a day off work to visit the vet, and so you'll probably need to arrange visits for evenings and weekends if your vet is available at those times. It's a good idea to check the operating hours of your local vet before deciding which one to use.

If your TT just needs a regular checkup or some shots, make the appointment well in advance so that you know you can get booked without issue. If you take your TT to his vet at regular intervals, it can prevent the need to take him unexpectedly in the future.

Photo Courtesy
of Mr and Mrs C. Davies

Photo Courtesy of Caron Kay

Hire a Reliable Pet-Sitter

If you are required to spend long hours away from home for work, it can be very unfair to your TT. As mentioned in previous chapters, he will get bored very quickly and almost certainly become destructive if he suddenly finds himself alone for hours on end.

If you're often away from home, consider hiring a pet-sitter to keep your dog company during the day. There are plenty of resources for online pet sitting services, including rover.com and petsitter.com, where you'll find verified sitters in your local area. If you know of any trustworthy local teenagers, you'll find them very willing to earn a little extra money, especially if they get time to spend with your adorable TT!

Consider Hiring a Dog Walker

If you work long hours and have a TT, it's important he gets his daily walks whether you feel up to it or not. Some single TT parents find it easier to hire a dog walker to take him out for a good long walk on the days they're away from home. You'll be able to find a local dog walker from the same services mentioned above that offer pet-sitting. They are available on an app to make things even easier.

Assign an Emergency Pet Caretaker

It's vital that you take some precautionary measures in case you have a medical emergency. It's not a case of being over-dramatic either. Rather it is being prepared for any eventuality. Talk to a trusted friend or neighbor about being a first responder for your dog in any crisis. If you are stuck at work, suddenly need to go to the hospital, or have some other kind of emergency, it will give you huge peace of mind knowing your TT is in the best of hands.

How about Doggy Daycare?

If your circumstances permit, doggy daycare is a fantastic way of ensuring your TT is happy as Larry while you're at work. Daycare centers are specifically set up to take care of dogs for daytime sessions and have scheduled activities that can be excellent for your TT's development. Doggy daycare providers take care of meals and walks, and if your dog has any kind of emergency, the staff can get him to the vet and let you know immediately.

Photo Courtesy of Julie Burg

Schedule Grooming Sessions

When you're a lone TT parent, you have to make sure you get a groomer who can work around your schedule. Your TT's going to need regular attention when his double coat is fully grown. If you're on your own, it's hard to find the time you need to dedicate to your TT's grooming, especially as he really enjoys a luxurious spa experience. Book grooming sessions in advance so that you know his needs are taken care of. You'll find more detailed information about grooming TTs in Chapter 14.

Get Pet Products Delivered

You can get almost everything from pet food to pet meds delivered to your door on a regular basis. Going to physical pet stores to get everything you need is difficult to fit into a busy work schedule. It's always a good idea to purchase everything online with doorstep delivery so that you have more time to dedicate to your new companion.

Photo Courtesy of Amanda Green

Second Pet

Although this will sound completely insane to some, getting another pet as a companion for your lone TT is actually a great idea. Make sure you have really gotten to know your TT before introducing another dog or cat. You want to know you can handle everything with your first canine charge before accepting another animal into your fold.

Essentially, it's not terribly difficult being a single TT parent as long as you are organized and have planned ahead. The upside is that you and your TT will develop a relationship that exists on a completely different level than if he were living in a family unit. As a single TT parent, he is your roommate, companion, furry dependent, and even a fantastic excuse to stay in on a Friday night!

HELPFUL TIP
Do They Shed?

Tibetan Terriers are low-shedding dogs and are considered a hypoallergenic breed. You may notice heavier-than-average shedding twice a year during seasonal changes, but overall, you can expect minimal shedding year-round. Despite being light shedders, Tibetan Terriers need frequent grooming to avoid tangles in their luscious locks.

Avoiding Separation Anxiety

TTs develop such close relationships with humans that they can easily experience anxiety when left alone. This is something that particularly affects single TT parents, as there's less likely to be at least one person in the house throughout the day. Separation anxiety is more than just whining a little when you leave or acting out when you've gone: it is a serious condition and a common source of frustration that leads to TTs being given up. There's no need to despair, however; there are plenty of things you can do to help your dog cope with long periods alone, without feeling any anxiety at all.

First, you should understand the kind of things that might cause him to behave this way:

- Perhaps he is being left alone for the first time, having gotten used to being with people.
- There's been a change of ownership.
- He's moved from a shelter into your home.
- He's suffered the loss of a family member.

Signs of Separation Anxiety

When a TT has separation anxiety, he will show a lot of stress when left alone, including:

- Howling, barking, or whining excessively
- Having "accidents" despite being house-trained
- Chewing things, scratching at windows and doors, and destroying furniture
- Panting, drooling, or salivating much more noticeably than usual
- Pacing obsessively
- Attempting to escape.

Although many TTs will do some of these things some of the time, if your dog has separation anxiety, he will do them almost all the time when he's alone.

Photo Courtesy of Helen Baker

How to Treat It

As with everything that seems wrong with your TT, you should first rule out any medical problems by consulting your vet. If he's having accidents when left alone, he could have an infection or a hormone problem, so you'll need to get that checked out before working on his separation anxiety as it might resolve the issue quickly.

If the Problem Is Mild:

- Give your dog a special treat every time you leave the house. Puzzle toys are fantastic for TTs as they appeal to a dog's curiosity, and if it's a toy stuffed with a treat like peanut butter, even better! If you have to leave for a while, leave a few puzzle toys stuff with different smelly treats to keep your dog amused when you're gone.

- Don't make a big deal out of leaving and returning. In fact, you should try ignoring your TT before you exit and for a few minutes after you've returned home. This will help him accept your schedule as part of his own, and he'll feel much more comfortable about the routine.

- Leave some of your clothes with your scent on them around. Your dog will take a lot of comfort from being able to smell you when you're not there.

- Consider getting your vet's advice about calming supplements or look for a natural over-the-counter product.

If the Problem Is More Serious:

Even the tastiest treats won't distract your TT if he has severe separation anxiety. In this situation, you'll have to slowly get him used to your absence.

Your TT is a master of reading the signs of when you're getting ready to leave, like picking up your keys or putting on your jacket. Try doing those things without leaving the room. Let him see that it doesn't necessarily signal you're going to leave him alone. Do this a few times during the day. This will stop him from getting nervous when he sees your exit is imminent.

When he has started to feel less anxious about things before you've even left the house, you can slowly start to disappear. At first, ask him to "stay" and stand just on the other side of the door, reappearing after a few seconds. Slowly increase the amount of time you're out of his sight and then introduce your normal behavior of picking up your keys and putting on your jacket each time you leave the room. Tell him to stay each time you leave, and he will slowly learn to become relaxed when you give him this instruction.

Whether he is ready to be left alone for longer periods is purely down to you because only you know him well enough. Don't rush it, though, as separation anxiety can be a stubborn problem. When you're slowly getting him used to your absence, give him a stuffed treat when you've achieved a goal, like spending 30 seconds apart and so on. Always stay calm when you leave the room and when you walk back through the door.

Photo Courtesy
of Mairi White

Use Exercise and Play to Relieve Stress

If you have to leave your TT alone for several hours every day, it's a good idea to walk him before you leave. When he's tired, he'll be less stressed, and that'll make it easier for you to leave your home. Because of your TTs endless curiosity, it's important that he have plenty of things to stimulate him when you're not around.

You need to work your dog's mind as well as his body! When you're with him, play training games and fetch, and when he's alone, use puzzle games and chews to keep him busy. If there's enough to occupy his mind while he's on his own, he will soon adapt to your absences so that you can have a guilt-free working day!

CHAPTER 12

Diet and Nutrition for Your Tibetan Terrier

> 66
>
> *Unlike people, dogs do better eating the same food all the time. Feed less than the bag instructs for your dog's weight. Dog food companies tend to recommend too much food, and dogs often become overweight. There should be no roll of fat behind the neck, at the top of the shoulder (the withers). A trim TT has more energy and finishes his dish at each meal. A 25 pound TT eats 1 1/2 cups of dry food per day, half in the morning and half at dinner. Limit treats to when you are training, and never feed your TT from the dining table.*
>
> JACKIE FAUST
> *Arkeden Tibetan Terriers*
>
> 99

In the same way we humans learn to feed ourselves a healthy diet, there's much more to choosing your dog food than you might imagine. In this chapter, we take a dive into the world of doggy diet and nutrition and the things you need to take into account when feeding your Tibetan Terrier.

We'll cover everything you need to know in the following ten points:

Know His Nutritional Needs

The first thing to understand is the right nutritional balance you want to achieve in your TT's diet. Here are the most important nutritional values he'll need to get from his food:

Photo Courtesy of Nicky Smith

Aminos & Fatty Acids

You'll be surprised to learn that dogs need 22 amino acids for survival, 12 of which they manufacture themselves. There are 10 amino acids that dogs can't synthesize themselves, which you should ensure are ALWAYS in your TT's food, including:

- Valine
- Histidine
- Lysine
- Melanin tryptophan.
- Leucine
- Isoleucine
- Threonine
- Arginine
- Methionine
- Phenylalanine

There are meat and plant sources for each of these amino acids, which can be found in the ultimate nutrition resource, the Exploratorium Science of Cooking Guide, widely available online.

Dogs are perfectly able to digest food from plant sources as well as they do meat. However, meat-based proteins are extremely efficient means of delivering these vital nutrients for conversion into protein. This is due to the similar structure of muscles in both humans and animals.

Proteins

Your TT needs lots of protein in his diet, mainly because they are the building blocks for organs, cells, and tissues, together with hormones, antibodies, and enzymes. Protein can be sourced from both meat and plant sources, and there is even a trend toward insect protein too.

Proteins are important for:

- Growth and healthy maintenance of muscle, hair, and nails
- Transporting nutrients through your TT's body
- Ensuring his immune system functions effectively
- Producing hormones for healthy development

When you choose food for your TT, the protein source should be first on the ingredient list and named. If you can see "beef," "chicken," or "salmon" at the top of the list, it is a good indicator of quality. If the protein source is listed as "meat by-products" or "poultry," this can mean any part of an animal is mixed in the bag of food.

 If your TT shows signs of developing a food allergy, try changing the main source of protein in his food as an initial step to discovering the problem.

Fats

Fats always sound as though they are really unhealthy, but we all need them as an essential energy source, including our dogs. The kinds of fats used in dog food are very digestible, which means they quickly provide an energy boost.

Fats are made up of fatty acids in a similar way to amino acids, which are the building blocks of protein. The two essential fatty acids your TT needs

*Photo Courtesy
of Juan Boria and Michael John*

in a balanced proportion in his food are omega-3 and omega-6. Dogs are unable to synthesize these fatty acids themselves.

Good sources of fatty acids include the following:

- Fish oils from herring, salmon, etc.
- Flaxseed oil
- Canola oils
- Sunflower oils
- Corn oils
- Soybean oils
- Pork fat or any poultry fat

Some surprising sources of fats you should include in your TT's diet are:

- Avocado
- Nut and seed butters
- Plant oils
- Whole eggs
- Fatty fish (salmon is ideal)
- Seeds such as flax, hemp, pumpkin, sunflower, chia, and sesame
- Full-fat yogurt

Fats in your TT's diet are absolutely essential. It's important to note that dogs are not at the same risk as humans of heart disease due to having too many saturated fats in their diet. However, you should be careful to balance fats in your TT's food so that he doesn't become overweight or less active.

 TIP *The label should list the kinds of fats included and at what levels. Look for specific mentions of omega-3 and omega-6.*

Vitamins & Minerals

Your TT's food should also contain small amounts of vitamins and minerals, including the following:

VITAMINS:

- A, C, D, E, and K
- B1, B6, B12
- Folic acid
- Riboflavin
- Niacin
- Pantothenic acid
- Choline

MINERALS:

- Calcium
- Phosphorous
- Iron
- Magnesium
- Sodium
- Potassium
- Chlorine
- Copper
- Manganese
- Selenium
- Iodine
- Zinc

Your TT's food should ideally contain the required daily amounts of vitamins and minerals. If he has too much or too little of the vital nutrients, he could develop health problems further down the line. If you feel your TT is not getting enough nutrition from his diet and are considering supplements, always consult your vet before taking it further.

Carbohydrates

We all know that carbs give you energy, and dogs are no exception to this rule. Carbohydrates also play an important role in your TT's intestinal health. One of the most beneficial carbs is fiber, which helps manage your TT's bowel movements and prevents diarrhea.

Carbohydrates are the first food source for energy, followed by proteins. Carbs are useful for providing an immediate energy boost so that your TT is primed to run after a ball or down a trail. While he's running on his carbs, he'll be conserving proteins for producing and maintaining his body tissues. The best fibers to consider when choosing your TT's food include brans from corn, rice, and wheat. It is really important to note that foods high in fiber should be limited for TTs with high energy levels and puppies.

> 🔅 **TIP** *The Association of American Feed Control Officials (AAFCO) is responsible for publishing guidelines on balanced nutrition in animal food. However, it still helps to understand the balance between amino acids, proteins, fats, vitamins, minerals, and carbohydrates and how they keep your TT healthy.*

Schedule Feedings

What food you should choose for your TT is just a small part of the story. How much and how often you feed him is just as important. Too much of a good thing can be, well...bad.

The food you buy for your dog will almost certainly have feeding guidelines on the packaging. But you should remember that they are just guidelines and not necessarily applicable for your TT. It depends on his activity level, how much he eats, and other factors only you'll be able to determine.

The best approach is to follow the feeding guidelines and keep an eye on your TT's weight. If he starts looking like a fatty, simply reduce the amount of food you give him. Be prepared for a little pushback on this from your

TT. That said, he'll stop complaining soon enough once he's adjusted to the new regime.

You should also feed your TT on a schedule and make his mealtimes the same every day. Dogs of all types love the security of routines, and they feel settled when everything happens as expected. Most people feed their TTs twice a day, once in the morning and again in the evening. If this doesn't fit your lifestyle or the energy output of your TT, you should make appropriate adjustments to the schedule.

If your TT develops a weight problem, consider switching to food that has a lower calorie formula. Make sure that there are still the correct nutrients in the food even though it has reduced calories. If you just feed your dog less of his usual food, he could become malnourished over time.

There are several increased risks for overweight and obese TTs, including:

- Osteoarthritis and hypertension
- Some types of cancer
- Metabolic and endocrine disorders such as type 2 diabetes and renal dysfunction
- Reduced quality of life
- Reduced life expectancy
- Inflammation in joints and internal systems

Life Stage Is Important

Some dog foods state that they are "balanced for all ages," which, although convenient, may not be the best for your TT. There is a big difference between the nutritional requirements of a puppy compared to a senior TT, and your dog should be fed according to those needs.

Here is what your TT will need in his food throughout the different life stages:

- **Puppies:** Food should support your dog's growth and include at least 25% of a single source of protein such as chicken, tuna, lamb, beef, or turkey. Take note of the portion guidelines on the packaging, keeping in mind the risks of overfeeding puppies, which can cause health issues later on.
- **Adults:** When your TT is fully grown, he can be less active than he was as a puppy or equally as rambunctious. Generally speaking, your adult

TT will require less protein and fat in his diet. There are lots of factors you need to consider when deciding on your TT's portions, including:

- His activity level—The more energetic he is, the more food he'll need. If he's a lapdog, he'll need less.

- Outdoor temperature—When your TT needs to warm up or cool down, he'll burn more calories and energy, so he'll most likely need more food.

- Exercise regime—If you and your TT regularly step out together for a long hike or jog around the park, you might want to up his protein and carb intake to give him the energy he needs.

- **Senior TTs (7+ years):** Your older TT will still need proteins to help him maintain muscle mass. Even old TTs get the occasional burst of energy, and he'll need the right nutritional balance to help him. His metabolic rate is likely to decrease as he ages, which can sometimes lead to weight gain. It's a good idea to choose food with the following ingredients for your older boy. They help maintain good gut health:

  - Gamma-linolenic acid (GLA), a fatty acid that will help keep your TT's skin and coat looking fabulous

  - Fructooligosaccharides (FOS), which helps promote the production of beneficial bacteria and prevent gastrointestinal disease

  - Vitamin E and beta-carotene, which gets rid of tissue-damaging bacteria that causes signs of aging

 As your TT transitions from puppy to adult to senior, introduce age-appropriate foods slowly over a few days. Some TTs can react to a sudden change in diet by vomiting, so you want to take your time.

Mix Wet & Dry Foods

One of the most common questions relating to choosing the right dog food is whether to go for wet or dry food. The advantage of canned foods is that they contain at least 75% moisture and have a taste that appeals to dogs. Kibble, on the other hand, is really cost-effective, convenient, and great for your TT's oral health as the pellets scrape food off his teeth.

Feeding your TT is all about getting a balance between price and nutrition, so it's worth considering mixing wet and dry foods together to get the best from both. Find a good-quality wet food that your TT loves to chow down on and mix a couple of spoonfuls with his regular kibble.

There are a few considerations for mixing wet food with dry food, including:

- There is more water in wet food, which is essential for all TTs but particularly those with kidney problems or bladder stones.

Photo Courtesy
of Hannah Howard

- Kibble is excellent for dental hygiene, with the hard pellets scraping loose food from your TT's teeth.

- Wet food is much more tasty and appealing for your TT than dry food and can help a picky eater clear his bowl.

- Wet food should be refrigerated as soon as it's opened and must be used within a few days.

- Start with a small amount of wet food mixed in with kibble and see how much your TT finishes in one sitting. You should never leave wet food to sit out all day.

- If you're uncertain about wet food, you can always add moisture, nutrients, and taste to kibble with a wet topper such as a spray or bone broth.

- If you're serving kibble on its own, pour a little water over it to add moisture and introduce more water at feeding time.

One concern about feeding your TT wet food alone is the negative impact it can have on his teeth. If you mix wet and dry food, he'll still get the hard crunch of kibble to help clean his teeth.

 The nutritional values of wet and dry foods are different. The main difference is the amount of water in the product. It's important to read the labels on each type of food to get a good understanding of the nutritional value of each.

Learn about Grains

Grains are often promoted as a way to keep fatty carbs out of pet foods and are an excellent source of carbs, which provide your TT with energy, as covered above. It's also important to consider whole grains as a good source of fiber for your TT.

If your TT is not very active or is getting on in years, you should look for food with lower carb content than grain-free. The analysis labels on packaging should show you how many carbohydrates your TT will get per serving, which is a better indication than just opting for any type of grain-free food.

Some people are concerned that their dogs might develop allergies to grains in a way similar to humans. However, although dogs can be allergic to food, grain allergies are very rare, and allergies are more likely to be related to the protein source, such as beef, chicken, or dairy.

Your TT can get some valuable nutrients from whole grains, including vitamins, fatty acids, fiber, and minerals. The most common grains included in dog food are:

- Rice
- Oats
- Corn
- Barley
- Wheat

If you're considering grain-free food for your TT, make sure that you see what the grain has been replaced with. Is it peas or potatoes or a less nutritious filler? If you want to eliminate grains from your TT's diet, make sure the food you get has quality ingredients and a balanced composition.

Know What to Avoid

Your TT has the most appealing set of eyes, and when he wants something, he knows he can easily melt your heart and make you relent. However, when you're sitting down to eat, and you can feel those eyes burning holes in you, it's important to know what your dog can't eat when it comes to human food.

Here is a list of several foods that you should NEVER give to your TT:

1. **Chocolate:** Toxic to your TT, chocolate can cause vomiting, diarrhea, heart problems, tremors, and seizures.

2. **Dairy Products:** Cheeses and milk-based products can cause diarrhea, which leads to dehydration.

3. **Almonds:** These nuts are an obstruction hazard that can cause heart disease. They can also lead to pancreatitis, a painful condition that causes vomiting, diarrhea, and weight loss.

4. **Raisins or grapes:** These carry a risk of kidney failure.

5. **Raw eggs:** These can lead to food poisoning, including salmonella and skin problems.

6. **Raw fish:** These contain enzymes that are toxic to dogs and can lead to seizures and even death.

7. **Bread dough:** The enzymes in yeast can create CO_2 and ethyl alcohol and, when absorbed into the bloodstream, can cause respiratory failure.

Research Dog Food Brands

Where is your chosen brand of dog food manufactured? Where does it source the proteins in the food? How does the company guarantee the quality of the ingredients?

Photo Courtesy of John Pattinson

TT parents ask many more questions about the ingredients in their best buddy's food than previous generations. All brands should be completely transparent about where they source ingredients and manufacture their food. You should be able to find this information on a product page by googling the brand name to find the company's website, where you'll probably also find customer reviews.

Of course, it's not easy doing this kind of research, but if your TT is showing some kind of reaction to his food, it can help you figure out the causes. Unless your TT is doing very poorly, it's always a good idea to check his food before taking him to the vet to figure out what the problem is. Dogs are generally very quick to react physically to something they've eaten that disagrees with them, so it should be easy to detect a link.

 TIP *If you can't find the information you're looking for from your TT's food brand, switch to one that is more transparent immediately.*

Feed Well on Any Budget

It's a fallacy to believe that you can only feed your TT well if you're prepared to spend a little extra. It doesn't necessarily follow that a more expensive food will be more nutritious. The packaging may cost more to produce, or the company may source proteins from overseas. It's very easy

HELPFUL TIP
Patellar Luxation

Tibetan Terriers can be genetically predisposed to develop patellar luxation, a disorder affecting the knee, more common in small dog breeds. Patellar luxation occurs when the patellar ligament attached to the knee pops out of place when the dog's knee is extended. This condition has several levels of severity and may worsen with a dog's age. Signs that your dog is dealing with a luxating patella may include a noticeable hiccup in your dog's gait or seeing your dog run briefly on three legs and then return to regular running. This disorder can sometimes be corrected with surgery.

to be deceived into believing that a dog food is of better quality than it actually is.

There are so many options available: dry kibble, wet canned, freeze-dried, and even raw. As mentioned above, dry food is often the most practical choice in terms of price and shelf-life. You often pay a premium for wet food, and it also has to be refrigerated as soon as it's opened. Freeze-dried and raw foods are the most expensive of all, and there is still controversy over this kind of diet. So with that in mind... how can you feed your TT well on a budget?

As mentioned before, the best way to stretch your budget is to mix dry food with wet. However, there are some other ways you can balance nutrition and reduce costs:

- Spray krill over kibble to add omega-3s.
- Freeze bone broth in ice cube trays, defrost before feeding time, and pour over dry food to make it tastier and add nutrients.
- Occasionally integrate raw foods, many of which are comparably priced with some canned foods.
- Add raw meat scraps you've bought from the grocery store to your dog's diet, including things like chicken gizzards, hearts, livers, and chunks of venison or beef.
- You can liven up your TT's kibble by adding raw or blanched veggies, including carrots, broccoli, green beans, or peppers.

Find Expert Guidance

The Association of American Feed Control Officials (AAFCO) has established the basic nutritional and labeling requirements for dog foods. They are the regulators of the pet food industry that ensures brands are not able to make illegitimate claims. Another agency regulating the labeling of food is the Food and Drug Administration (FDA). You can read more about the latest guidelines by visiting their respective websites.

Both these groups govern the accuracy of how food is described and how much of its ingredients must be included, such as:

- A food claiming to be "dinner" or "platter" or "entrée" must have at least 25% of the named ingredient

- Foods stating the product comes "with" a specific ingredient only needs to contain 3% of it

- Foods that are "flavored" just need a trace of that ingredient on the label.

Read the Label

The previous point leads us seamlessly to the last: read the label on your TT's food. Ingredients are listed by weight. The first item on the list is the dominant ingredient of the food. With wet food that has lots of moisture, water is likely to be at the top of the list. With kibble, which has had the water removed, the more nutritionally dense ingredients are further down the list.

You should see the ingredients in the dog food label in the following order:

- Protein source—look for a single source such as chicken or beef

- Organs such as liver and lung (sounds delicious, right?)

- Grains and vegetables.

The definitions of certain aspects of dog food labels need some translating. Here are some of the phrases used on dog foods and what they really mean:

- **Complete and Balanced:** The food contains more than 40 nutrients identified as essential to pet health by the AAFCO.

- **Life Stage:** Proteins, fats, carbs, and other nutrients have been adjusted to meet a specific stage of your TT's life, from puppy to adult to senior canine citizen.

- **Guaranteed Analysis:** The product information has been submitted to regulators and complies with nutritional requirements and label claims. This analysis covers protein, fat, fiber, and moisture levels.

- **Ingredients:** Although you might think this is obvious, the ingredients should also identify nutritional content, tastiness, digestibility, and whether the food contains any special vitamins and minerals.

CHAPTER 13

Grooming Your Tibetan Terrier

When you have a Tibetan Terrier in your life, grooming is a huge part of life. That's mainly because of the characteristic double coat your dog has that not only gives him his unique appearance, but also requires considerable upkeep.

Tibetan Terriers require routine grooming. When your dog is young, you need to get him used to regular grooming. A full brush out twice or three times a week is best, along with bathing every one to two weeks. Never brush your dog's coat when it's dry; mist with a hydrating spray before pulling the brush through his locks.

Even if you keep your TT in a shorter trim, you should give him a brush out at least once a week, with baths every one to four weeks. It's not advisable to wait until your dog's coat is matted before you groom him. Tibetan Terriers are a breed that requires you to stay on top of routine maintenance.

Your Tibetan Terrier's Unique Double Coat

> *Tibetan terrier's have a double coat and they need to be bathed and groomed often. Spend time brushing and training your puppy to enjoy it is vitally important because they will have to have it done the rest of their lives!*
>
> MAUREEN DWYER
> *Yonpo Tibetan Terriers*

Tibetan Terriers have a dense undercoat with a long silky topcoat. This is the main reason your dog will need a fair amount of brushing so that he

Photo Courtesy of Helen Baker

remains mat-free and in tip-top condition. Your TT will need regular groom-ing to remove dead hair from his undercoat and prevent matting. It's entirely up to you whether you keep him in a short trim, although it's just as easy to maintain a longer topcoat with regular brushing.

It's really important to get the correct products to match your TT's needs so that he enjoys the grooming experience while maintaining a healthy coat. Here, we'll dive into the grooming specifics for your TT that will maximize the beauty of his luxurious coat.

The Recommended Tools

It's useful to know exactly what equipment is required for grooming your TT, particularly as the range of brushes, combs, and scissors available is huge and confusing. It's important to use the right tools for the job because if your dog's coat becomes tangled or is in poor condition, grooming can quickly become a painful process for him.

Photo Courtesy
of Michelle Simmons

Here are some of the tools you'll need and what they're used for:

SLICKER BRUSH

This is used for brushing through your TT's coat and can be used on a daily basis. There are a few different types of slick brushes that have different types of bristles, including soft and hard. If your TT has a thicker double coat, it's probably better to opt for the hard slicker brush.

COMB

After you have brushed your TT through with a slicker brush, you can then use a comb to remove any remaining tangles. Check your TT's tail, back legs, ears, and chest areas for any knots, as they are particularly prone to matting. If your TT is very matted or tangled, don't attempt to comb through the knots, as this will be painful for him. It's a better idea to go to a groomer and get his coat trimmed short. You can also use a comb with scissors if you are trimming your TT's topcoat or cutting out any stubborn tangles.

FURMINATOR

This is a tool that helps you get rid of loose dead hair in your TT's undercoat. This will remove any excess hair that can become irritating to him and also prevent mats from developing.

NAIL CLIPPERS

Your TT needs to have his nails clipped regularly using pet nail clippers. Many people don't feel comfortable doing this, as you need to be sure you don't cut the "quick," which supplies blood to the nail, as this can cause the dog pain. For this reason, many people feel more comfortable taking their dogs to the vet or groomer to clip their nails. If you are happy to do the job yourself, invest in some clippers that are of good quality and introduce clipping to your TT on a regular basis.

You can make the whole process of trimming your TT's nails easier by following these steps:

The first time you clip your TT's nails, work with extreme caution. He may resist you, so it may be safer to have someone to help you initially until your dog learns to accept having his nails clipped. Work slowly and gently, talking softly to him to reassure him as you carefully and systematically trim each nail.

- Hold his paw firmly but gently.
- If he has translucent nails, and you can easily see the inner quick, clip off the transparent tips, making sure to avoid the quick. If he has dark-colored nails, and you can't see the quick, err on the side of caution and just trim the tips of his nails.
- If you do happen to nick the quick and his nail starts to bleed, apply pressure with some gauze or cotton wool to stop the bleeding. You can use styptic powder or solution to stop the bleeding quickly, so have some on hand in just in case.
- After trimming all the nails on one of his paws, you can file the rough edges with a nail file to get a neat finish.
- Repeat the above steps on all his paws until you've completed his pedicure.
- Tibetan Terriers have four dewclaws which are sometimes removed when they are puppies. If your TT still has two dewclaws on his front legs and two on the back, don't forget to check them when trimming his nails. Dewclaws don't wear down as readily, but they can cause problems if they do.
- When you've finished trimming your TT's nails completely, don't forget to shower him with praise and treats for being such a good boy.

You should make sure your dog's nails are clipped regularly using nail clippers. If you do not feel comfortable doing this, then take your dog to a vet or groomer to get it done. Your dog's nails can be dangerous and could cause him injury if they get too long. Invest in some nail clippers and get into the habit of clipping your dog's nails regularly.

HAIR-THINNING SCISSORS

Thinning scissors are similar to the ones used in hair salons to reduce volume in very thick hair. Thinning scissors have irregular teeth, which gently remove strands of hairs so as to thin out your TT's coat in areas where it is a little thick and requires basic styling.

UNDERCOAT RAKE

If your TT's coat has become really thick, you can use an undercoat rake to get to the hair underneath his silky topcoat. Undercoat rakes get really deep into the dog's coat where other brushes can't reach and are helpful in removing knots and excess hair.

Photo Courtesy of Kelli Murphy

EASIDRI DOG TOWEL

Easidri dog towels are really effective for drying off your TT, rather than using several towels for one drying session. Easidri towels are ultra-absorbent and will help you dry your TT much quicker than a regular towel, which will reduce your grooming time too.

WHERE TO GROOM

It's really up to you where you decide to groom your TT, although it's good to have a dedicated space. Ideally, you should groom him on a grooming table that has a non-slip surface. That said, you can get creative and groom him on top of your washing machine or any surface where he won't slide around. You can always use a bath mat with a non-slip underside for your dog to stand on for his security.

Grooming Your Tibetan Terrier Puppy

> *Start the grooming process at a young age. As a puppy, bath them weekly in the kitchen sink. They may not need the bath but it helps get them used to the process when it only takes a short amount of time. To prepare them for brushing when they have more hair, as a puppy start laying them on their sides and just give them a quick massage. Don't forget to play with their toes to help desensitize them for clipping or grinding later. And remember to praise and reward for desired behaviors!*
>
> RENE' STAMM
> *Euphoria Tibetans*

Your TT puppy's coat is relatively easy to manage because he won't have a full topcoat until around 18 months. Despite the fact he won't need so much grooming, it's still a good idea to get into the habit of it, as he'll need to get used to regular sessions as he gets older. This will help him adjust to grooming as part of his normal life, and he may even find the experience enjoyable.

It's best to start with short sessions, as your pup only has a short attention span. Lightly spray him with a hydrating mix of conditioner and water and brush him with the pin brush in the direction of hair growth. Just spend

Photo Courtesy
of Donna Campbell

FUN FACT
Long-Lived Dogs

Tibetan Terriers have an average lifespan of around 12 to 15 years. However, a man in Leicester, England, claims to have had the oldest Tibetan Terrier mix. The dog's name was Bertie, and he turned 21 on January 29, 2010. Bertie's owner rescued the pup when he was five years old. The Guinness World Record for the oldest dog is held by an Australian Cattle Dog named Bluey, who lived an impressive 29 years.

a few minutes with this, and see if you can get him to lie on his side so that you can really groom him thoroughly.

Get your TT pup used to being handled and touched with brushes and combs. Always be gentle and use soothing tones in your voice if he is nervous. Most of all, remain patient. Try and develop a routine for grooming so that as you prepare your tools and nonslip surface, your dog will know what's coming next.

It's a good idea to get your TT pup used to all the things he will experience when he is an adult. Although it might not be time to bathe him, you might want to give him a quick once-over occasionally to get him used to the experience. Make sure that the water is neither too hot nor too cold before you get your puppy wet. Afterward, it might be easier for you to let him dry out naturally but also get him used to a blow dryer, even if only for very short bursts.

Your pup should get used to having his toenails cut, which many dogs— and dog parents—don't particularly enjoy. Nail clippers can seem like a nasty-looking tool for your baby TT, so you might have to give him a treat to distract him on the first go. While he's enjoying the treat, you can cut one toenail and then the following day, cut another until they are all clipped. As with all puppy training, patience and consistency are the best approaches.

Grooming Your Adolescent Tibetan Terrier

As your TT gets older, his coat will start to change. This period can last anywhere from a few weeks to several months. During this time, you'll have to groom him frequently as mats and dead hair are more prolific and can develop overnight.

At around ten months, your TT's coat will start to transform, so he should be already primed for regular grooming by this point. During this coat change, his coat is likely to shed every single day for around three weeks, which will require considerable attention to avoid problematic matting.

Photo Courtesy
of Renè Stamm

Grooming Your Adult Tibetan Terrier

Ideally, your adult TT should be bathed an average of every seven to 10 days, with a good grooming session at the same time. If you keep your TT in a short trim or puppy cut, he can be bathed less frequently. That said, there are plenty of TT owners who have their dogs professionally bathed and groomed once a month, with maintenance brushing in the interim. Both your lifestyle and that of your TT will dictate how regularly you need to groom him.

Here are some steps for bathing your TT:

- When giving your TT a bath, always put him in a tub that has a nonslip surface. Although you can get his coat wet by pouring water over him, it's often easier to use a hand-held showerhead or a spray attachment for your faucet.

- Get your dog completely wet down to his skin. If you're using a spray attachment, try to keep the water running in the same direction that the hair is growing, with downward strokes. If you spray upward, it is very likely to cause tangles.

- Once your dog is completely wet, pour some good-quality shampoo over his coat. Really work the shampoo into his coat without rubbing or scrubbing at his skin because this will cause more tangles. Some shampoos need to be left on for a minute or so before rinsing. It is not advisable to use human shampoo on your TT, as it will disrupt the acid mantle, which will leave him vulnerable to parasites, viruses, and bacteria. It can also make a dog's skin feel dry and flaky, which can lead to repeated scratching and abrasions.

- When rinsing, take care to spray water in the direction of your dog's hair in the same way as above. Make sure you get all the soapy bubbles out of his fur. You should feel that his coat is squeaky clean after rinsing, without any residue shampoo.

- Follow with conditioner in exactly the same way.

- When your TT is rinsed thoroughly, squeeze any excess water out of his coat by running your hands down his legs, down his tail from root to tip, and down his ears. Don't squeeze too tightly, obviously. Then you can place a towel over his back and begin to blot (don't rub) any excess water out of his coat.

- When your dog is washed and blotted, he's ready for the grooming table. Start brushing with your pin brush while blow-drying him at the same time. Blow the dryer in the same direction as his hair grows, while brushing him the same way. As you're brushing your TT, you might need to clip his hair out of the way so that you can really get into his undercoat.

- Brush his legs first and then go to his belly. Where you can, part your dog's hair and then brush out the hair below, again in the direction that it grows. Remove any mats and tangles as you find them, and comb through each section when you've finished brushing. Continue parting and brushing like this until you have brushed all the way up your TT.

- When brushing, hold the brush loosely. If you have a tight grip, you'll risk tearing through your dog's coat. To remove a mat, lightly spray with grooming spray or diluted conditioner and try to separate the tangle with your fingers or tease it with a comb. If you can separate mats into smaller clumps, they are easier to remove with your comb.

- You can use a comb as a way of locating any mats you have missed. If it catches somewhere, you can easily find the source of the tangle. Mats generally develop at certain friction points, like under the chin or on a dog's chest, his elbows, his tail, and under his belly.

Other Dematting Ideas

Most tangles in your TT's coat should be able to be removed with a combination of your fingers, a comb, and brush. However, there are bound to be times when your TT develops a stubborn mat, and the usual methods don't work. Here are a few ideas to help you if you encounter this situation:

- Soaking the tangle in undiluted conditioner or oil allows mats to slip apart more easily. Just bear in mind that your TT will probably need another bath afterward to remove any residue.

- Look for products containing silicone or a natural alternative because they help mats slide out easily. Again, your dog might need a shampoo and rinse afterward.

- You can use a slicker brush to remove mats, although they can tear at your TT's coat and should be reserved for particularly stubborn tangles.

- If the worst comes to the worst and you still can't get rid of a mat, you can always resort to using scissors to break it up. Just be careful to point your scissors away from your TT and cut the mat out that way. Make sure you don't cut his skin, too, as it can be hard to know where a mat ends and your TT's body begins.

- Many TT owners find it easier to keep their dogs in a short trim so as to prevent any matting from occurring in the first place. This is obviously a matter of personal choice.

Why Grooming Is Important for Your Tibetan Terrier

> **"**
>
> *If you don't like brushing I would not get a coated breed. To me, the hair makes a Tibetan a Tibetan. However, it depends on the lifestyle you want with your dog and how much time you want to spend on them grooming. Some people find it as a great bonding time or even therapeutic sitting at night brushing. Keeping them in a shorter clip is very common and much easier to maintain for the busy lifestyles these days. Having a longer tail, beard, and ears is quite a common cut that requires far less brushing.*
>
> NIKKIE KINZIGER
> *Ri Lee Kennels*
>
> **"**

When you take your TT to a professional groomer, they carry out a seven-point check on him before picking up a brush. These checks include eyes, ears, skin, teeth, gums, ears, nails, and his bottom. Groomers often pick up on things that owners haven't noticed, like hidden wounds or parasites such as ticks.

Grooming is vital for keeping your TT in great condition, although many owners don't realize the connection to overall health. Grooming is not just about making him look like the bee's knees; it has a big effect on his health and quality of life. If not brushed frequently, your TT will be prone to developing all sorts of knots and tangles, sometimes very quickly. It's important to remember that Tibetan Terriers need a little more TLC in the grooming department than most other breeds.

Matting and dirt build-up can lead to your TT developing skin irritations, which can become more problematic over time. Fleas are a universal problem for all breeds but can be especially hard to spot in a TT's prolific coat, which is another reason to ensure he is regularly groomed. Consistent grooming will also stop your TT's hair from getting into his eyes and ears, which can lead to infections.

Keeping your TT's teeth clean is also an important part of his grooming, particularly for his dental health. Many owners find it easier to use dog chews that are specifically designed to care for canine teeth and gums. You can also find regular toothbrushes and toothpaste products available online or in pet stores, but if you find them difficult to source, your vet should be able to point you in the right direction.

CHAPTER 14

Traveling with Your Tibetan Terrier

Your Tibetan Terrier is the perfect size to be your traveling companion, and it's also a great bonding experience to hit the road with your favorite pooch. Here we take a closer look at how to get the maximum enjoyment for both you and your TT when you're taking him on trips with you.

Health and Safety

You should take your TT to your vet for a health checkup before you go on an extended trip. While you're there, you can make sure your dog's jabs are up to date, too, because you'll need to take his shot records with you on trips. Ask your vet if he feels your TT's mental and physical health is suited for traveling by airplane, train, ship, car, or whichever mode of transport you'll be using. You should bear in mind that although TTs love a good long hike on occasion, they aren't necessarily keen on other types of travel.

Photo Courtesy of Vivian Hawkins

To ensure your dog is healthy and happy while you're traveling, bring a supply of his usual food with you if it's an extended trip. Make sure you have plenty of bottled water and any medications the dog might need at the time.

In the same way as traveling with kids, you should be prepared for an emergency. Locate the nearest 24-hour emergency vet where you're staying, and put the number in your cell phone. You should also have your own vet's

Photo Courtesy of Julie Boncher

emergency number just in case both vets need to speak to each other about your TT's case.

CRATES

Using a crate is perhaps the best way to ensure your TT is safe in the car. A crate is a requirement for all airline travel. Crates can also prevent your TT from getting in trouble when you're staying at a hotel or a host's home.

Look for these features when purchasing a crate for your TT:

- Large enough for your TT to stand up, turn around, and lie down
- Sturdy with handles and grips to make it easily portable
- A leak-proof bottom, which you should cover with absorbent material
- Ventilation on opposite sides with exterior rims or dials to prevent blockages in the airflow
- "Live Animal" label with arrows showing the crate's upright position together with your name, address, and telephone number

Make the crate familiar to your TT with a comfy mat, his favorite toy, and a water bottle, and he's good to go.

Identification

You should be prepared in case you are separated from your TT while traveling. Here are some tips:

- Make sure he has a good leash and collar with an identification tag. The tag should have your dog's name, your name, and your telephone number. You can also include proof of rabies shots if you get a locket-style tag. If you are going away for more than just a few days, you should consider buying a collar and ID tag with details of where you're staying.
- Consider a permanent form of ID such as a microchip, which is a mandatory requirement in many European countries.
- Bring along a recent snapshot of your TT, as well as a copy of his health records showing recent shots.

Traveling By Car

Don't leave your puppy home when you run errands in the car; instead take them along whenever possible. This will help avoid a chronically carsick puppy. But be sure to always crate your dog in the car. A loose dog is a driver distraction. In an emergency like a car crash, a crate could save your dog's life!

JACKIE FAUST
Arkeden Tibetan Terriers

A car is probably the most convenient way of traveling with your TT. You should follow these steps to ensure maximum enjoyment for both of you:

- Get your TT used to traveling in the car with you by letting him sit in it with you without actually going anywhere. Slowly start going on short rides, extending the time you spend driving until he gets accustomed to traveling with you in your car.

Photo Courtesy
of Kelli Murphy

Photo Courtesy of Caron Kay

- Prevent carsickness by letting your TT travel on an empty stomach, but make sure he has access to water.

- Keep your car ventilated. If your TT is in a crate, you want to make sure he has plenty of airflow.

- If you're not using a crate, use a dog seat belt or car seat to keep him safe and secure.

- Although dogs seem to love it, it's really not a good idea to let your TT stick his head out of the window. Hair thrashing around his eyes can lead to injury!

- If you're driving an open truck, don't let your TT ride in the back, even if secured. He is too exposed, and it's extremely dangerous for him.

- Make sure you stop frequently to exercise your TT and give him the chance to relieve himself. Always clean up after your TT too.

- If you have children traveling with you, make sure they don't tease or annoy your TT when in the car.

- Absolutely never leave your TT unattended in a closed vehicle, even for the shortest of times. You wouldn't leave a child in that situation, and the same should apply to your dog. If you have to leave the car, make sure someone in your family can stay with the dog.

Flying

Traveling by plane requires a little more consideration. As mentioned above, you should consult your vet beforehand. A certification of health must be provided to the airline you're using within 10 days of traveling. You'll also be required to present rabies and vaccination certificates, and your TT has to be at least eight weeks old and weaned to get permission to fly.

Airlines make it very clear that the responsibility for verifying your TT's health and ability to fly rests with you. If your TT is particularly nervous, you should ask your vet if it might be better to tranquilize the dog before flying. Also, check what the temperatures are going to be at your flight's starting point and your destination, as it may be either too cold or too hot to be safe for your dog to travel.

Federal regulations prevent shipping of live animals as excess baggage or cargo if they are to be exposed to temperatures below 45 degrees Fahrenheit or over 85 degrees Fahrenheit for longer than four hours from departure to arrival, including connections.

Bear in mind that each airline will have its own set of regulations and services for pet transportation. For example, if your crate doesn't meet the airline's specific regulations, your TT might not be able to travel. However, some airlines will allow very small dogs—or TT pups—in the passenger cabin if your crate or carrier fits under the seat in front of you.

Photo Courtesy of Hannah Howard

Traveling by Train, Bus, or Boat

Adult TTs weigh in at 20 to 24 pounds, which means that you might be disappointed if you plan to travel by train or bus. Amtrak trains only permit dogs less than 20 pounds, and they also charge a $25 fee. Greyhound buses and other interstate bus companies do not allow dogs at all unless they are service dogs. Local rail and bus services have their own policies, which you should check before traveling.

Dogs frequently travel on cruise lines or ships, and a cruise is a good option for a vacation with your TT. He'll be able to bunk down with you in your cabin and can join you on deck during the day. However, it's always worth checking out the policies of the operator before making firm plans, just to find out exactly where you can and can't take your dog while on board.

Best Practices When Traveling with Your Tibetan Terrier

Plan bathroom breaks: Before you leave for your trip, teach your TT to relieve himself on different surfaces like concrete or gravel. This will get him used to different terrains while you're on your trip and make it easier to encourage him to relieve himself quickly wherever you are. Bring plenty of bags with you to clean up after him.

Bring games and toys: TTs get bored easily, and so you'll need to keep him occupied at times while you're on vacation. Take along his favorite puzzle toys, and get some new toys to keep him stimulated.

Pack food and water: It's always better to give your TT only bottled water while he's away from home. This will prevent him from getting an upset stomach. Invest in some collapsible travel bowls for him, too, and get him used to them a few days before you travel.

Photo Courtesy of Julie Thomas

Photo Courtesy of Alexandra Marckx

Overnight Stays with your Tibetan Terrier

If your trip involves overnight stays in a hotel or motel, there are some important things to bear in mind, such as:

- You should always find out ahead of booking which establishments allow dogs and if they have any size restrictions.

- If your TT is permitted to stay, ensure you respect other guests, staff, and the property.

- Your TT should be kept as quiet as possible.

- Don't leave your dog unattended, as he might start barking or destroying property if he feels neglected.

- Ask the manager where you are allowed to walk your TT and make sure you don't leave any mess behind.

- Remember that your TT is an ambassador for all other dog guests at the hotel or motel you're staying at. Don't let him spoil it for his furry friends.

- TT-proof the room! You know exactly the kind of thing that is going to tempt your TT into harmful behavior, such as electrical cords and heavy ornaments. Make sure everything is out of reach, and check under the furniture to make sure the previous guests didn't leave anything behind that your dog shouldn't get hold of.

Boarding Kennels

It won't always be possible for you to take your TT on trips. When you have to go away for an indeterminate time, you should consider finding someone to move into your home and take care of your TT for you. This also gives you complete peace of mind that your TT's routine hasn't been interrupted, which can trigger insecurities.

However, it's not always possible to find a trusted family member or neighbor to help out, which is when you should consider using local boarding services.

If you are taking your TT to a boarding kennel for the first time, you should stay with him a little while before leaving. Take along some familiar toys and treats, and if he's on a special diet, make the staff aware of his needs and bring some of his regular food with you. Make sure he's completely settled before you leave and get the staff to keep in touch with how your dog is doing.

Many boarding services offer a pick-up and drop-off service so that you don't have to arrange transportation, which saves a lot of aggravation.

Most importantly, be confident that the kennels will look after your dog well, and don't give in to any guilt feelings you have. When you go to pick up your TT, or he's dropped off by the kennel, the pure joy he'll express at seeing you again will wash away any bad feeling for both of you. Remember that boarding kennels are also a great opportunity for practicing socialization.

You can locate your closest boarding kennels that maintain professional standards by looking online at Care.com or with Yellow Pages at Yelp.com.

Pet Sitters

An alternative to boarding kennels is using a pet sitting service. You can either appoint someone you know and trust to come to your home and take care of your TT or find someone locally to do the job for you.

The advantage of a professional pet sitter include:

- Most professional sitters are trained in pet CPR and first aid.

- They should have a business license, insurance, and bonds and make client testimonials available to you.

- You can hire a pro pet sitter on an agreement or contract, which includes terms of payment, cancellation policies, a vet release form, and emergency contact details.

Your TT is more likely to be less stressed when he can stay in his own home and stick to his usual routine. Hiring a pet sitter to take care of him, also avoids him being exposed to other dogs at a boarding kennel and possible illnesses as a consequence.

You can find professional pet sitters in your area online at Wag.com or Rover.com.

CHAPTER 15

Healthcare for Your Tibetan Terrier

Vaccinations and Certifications

The following vaccinations are mandatory for your TT:

DHLPP (Canine Distemper Combo): There are three rounds of the canine distemper vaccination given to puppies. The first shot is between six to eight weeks, the second 10–12 weeks, and the final shot at 14–16 weeks, which is followed up every three years.

Rabies: Dogs over 16 weeks old are required to have a rabies vaccination. Younger TT pups should have two rounds of puppy starter vaccines,

Photo Courtesy of Deborah Stevenson

Photo Courtesy
of Nicky Smith

which prevent parvovirus, hepatitis, and distemper. Your adult TT will need a rabies vaccination every one to three years.

Bordetella (kennel cough): The Bordetella vaccine is recommended for pups by the time they are six weeks old, and then they are revaccinated annually.

Recommended Vaccinations: Many vets highly recommend giving dogs an annual influenza shot. Although this sounds unnecessary, canine influenza (also known as dog flu) is very contagious and can even be deadly for pups and dogs with weak immune systems.

Pet Insurance

It's impossible to anticipate what will happen in the future, and there's no way of predicting when your TT will get sick or injured or how much it will cost to treat him. This is one of the biggest reasons you should consider pet insurance because it protects against unexpected vet expenses to give you peace of mind. There aren't many people who can afford a $1500 emergency vet bill, which is why it's important to consider pet insurance.

To fully understand how cost-effective pet insurance can be, you should know the kind of expenses that most dog owners face. Here are some of the routine expenses every TT parent faces:

- According to the American Society for the Prevention of Cruelty to Animals (ASPCA), dog parents spend around $355 to $650 annually on food, toys, treats, and other miscellaneous costs, depending on location.

- More infrequent purchases like bags, crates, cages, and baskets cost an additional $470 to $560, bringing the total first-year costs of owning a TT up to around $1,000 to $2,000.

- The average cost of a routine vet checkup can vary widely from $50 to $250 and won't include the cost of any medication if required.

- Vaccines are a more affordable expense at around $100 for your TT's core shots.

However, when considering pet insurance, it isn't the routine vet visits you should be concerned about when assessing your expenses. For a start, if your TT comes down with an illness that's diagnosed during a routine health check, you can expect his bills to grow from that point on. The most significant costs are always those you can't prepare for, such as unexpected surgeries or emergencies, which is why pet insurance can really be a lifesaver.

Tibetan Terrier-Specific Health Risks

If you're wondering whether the cost of pet insurance is worth it, it's worth considering the health risks that could potentially increase vet costs significantly as your TT gets older.

Like all breeds of dogs, Tibetan Terriers can have a propensity for certain health conditions, including the following:

- **Progressive Retinal Atrophy (PRA):** This is a degenerative condition that can cause blindness due to damage to the retina at the back of the eye. The good news is that it is possible to detect PRA several years before any sign of blindness. TTs are also extremely good at learning to compensate for disabilities and are still capable of leading a happy life even if they become blind.

- **Lens Luxation:** This is a genetic disorder that affects the eye by shifting the position of the lens in the eye. This displacement can be either partial or complete and is often treatable when caught early with meds or surgery. However, serious cases of lens luxation may require the dog's eye to be removed.

- **Hip Dysplasia:** Hip dysplasia occurs when the TT's femur isn't snugly fitted into the hip's pelvic socket. Sometimes this condition can exist without any physical signs or symptoms, whereas in other cases, there can be pain and lameness in one or both rear legs. It is possible to screen TTs for hip dysplasia, which is important as your dog can develop arthritis as he ages, which exacerbates the problem. If your TT is showing signs of hip dysplasia, you should get your vet to check him out. Female TTs with hip dysplasia should not be bred as there is an increased risk of birthing problems. Medication or surgery can be helpful if hip dysplasia interferes with your TT's quality of life.

Your TT's breed-specific risks of certain illnesses or chronic conditions are important factors when you're considering budgeting for the costs of keeping him healthy.

Photo Courtesy of Jess Kenny

How Pet Insurance Works

Pet insurance is reimbursement-based. That means when you have to take your TT to the vet because he's injured or sick, you pay your vet's bill and then submit a claim to your insurers for reimbursement. With pet insurance, you are able to use any vet you like as long as they are qualified, recognized, and certified.

Like car insurance, most pet insurance plans have:

- Deductibles
- Copays or partial reimbursement
- Annual or per-claim maximums
- Waiting periods

Many pet insurance policies are flexible and allow you to personalize certain aspects of your TT's plan so that it best suits your budget and his requirements.

What Does Pet Insurance Cover?

You should shop around and check the small print before committing to pet insurance, as coverage can vary widely between insurers. In general, your TT's insurance policy should include the following:

- Coverage for treatment costs for accidents, illnesses, and diseases
- Surgery, hospitalization, and specialist care
- Diagnostic and imaging tests, such as X-rays, MRIs, etc.

Some insurance companies also provide coverage for:

- TT breed-specific and genetic conditions
- Consultation fees
- Complementary or holistic treatments
- Chronic or recurring conditions like allergies, arthritis, etc.
- Prescribed medications
- ER treatment.

It's worth taking extra time to research pet insurance providers and check the small print to make sure it's a cost-effective expense.

Worms, Ticks, and Other Parasites

There are many forms of parasites in dogs, and they all have one thing in common: they often have a negative impact on your TT's health. Parasites can cause a great deal of discomfort, too, with symptoms ranging from mild irritation to serious illness.

Here's an overview of the most commonly found parasites in dogs, how they work, and the kind of problems they can cause.

Firstly, what is a parasite? According to the Centers for Disease Control and Prevention, they are "organisms that live on or in a host organism and get their food from or at the expense of its host."

Internal Parasites

HEARTWORMS

The heartworm is an internal parasite that enters a dog's bloodstream when the canine is bitten by an infected mosquito. The worms then mature in the dog's heart, sometimes growing to a sickening one foot in length, which forms a dangerous obstruction. Inflammation in the wall of the dog's heart disrupts blood flow, which makes the heart have to work much harder than it normally would. Once blood flow slows to a certain point, the dog develops a mild but persistent cough. He may also become fatigued after just a small amount of exercise and may show signs of appetite loss. Heartworms can lead to heart failure if not eliminated.

Photo Courtesy of Barb Forrester

The main problem with heartworms is that dogs generally don't display any symptoms prior to the parasite being detected via screening. This is a big reason for ensuring your TT has regular health checks, particularly as it is only possible to detect adult heartworms. Nevertheless, timing is of the essence, and your vet will be able to talk you through the right solutions for your TT.

Heartworm treatment is expensive and can take a toll on the dog, which means it must only be administered by a vet. In some cases where the heartworm has grown to a sizeable extent, it can only be removed surgically.

Fortunately, there are lots of preventative options for heartworm, including daily and monthly tablets and chewables.

HOOKWORMS

Hookworms are intestinal parasites that live inside a dog's digestive system, stealing nutrients for their own growth. These parasites can be acquired by a puppy from its mother, or if an adult dog swallows the parasite's eggs, or it burrows into the skin. Hookworm is an especially tricky parasite because the larvae live in the soil. This means they can easily be ingested when a dog comes into contact with them directly or by licking himself clean.

When the hookworm has attached itself to the intestinal wall, it feeds

on the blood. This can cause serious blood loss, which can have serious effects on puppies. The main problem caused by hookworms is anemia, which will make your TT extra tired and listless. Other symptoms of hookworms include diarrhea and weight loss. Your vet is easily able to detect hookworm from a stool sample, and infection can be prevented by keeping your TT's space scrupulously clean.

Photo Courtesy of Karen Dean

RINGWORM

Despite its name, ringworm is a fungus and not a worm. TT pups that are less than 12 months old are particularly susceptible to ringworm. If an adult dog is malnourished or has reduced immunity, he will also be vulnerable to ringworm, which is extremely transmissible.

As with other types of fungal problems, there are special shampoos and ointments available from vets that kill ringworm if the case is only mild. Oral medications are more likely to be required for more serious cases, and the dog's fur will need to be clipped very short.

ROUNDWORM

Roundworms are another very common parasite that usually appears in younger pups. Roundworms look like white strips of spaghetti, and they're around one to three inches long. You will see signs of roundworms in your TT's stool, as they are generally easy to spot. However, you should take a sample to your vet for confirmation. Symptoms of roundworms include coughing, diarrhea, weight loss, or vomiting. You should note that roundworms can infect children as well as other dogs.

TAPEWORM

Tapeworms can be ingested by dogs via a host that is harboring the parasite's eggs, usually a flea. Tapeworms will cause noticeable changes in your TT, including dramatic weight loss and diarrhea. If your TT has a tapeworm, you'll be able to see segments of what look like grains of rice around his anus area or in his stool. Your vet will be able to treat your TT with highly effective medication administered orally or by injection. The best prevention from tapeworm is to ensure your TT is free of fleas and kept away from dead animals or rotting garbage.

WHIPWORM

Whipworms can be acquired when a dog licks or sniffs contaminated ground. An adult whipworm is less than half an inch long and looks like a piece of fine thread. They live in the large intestine, but unlike other parasites, they are harder to detect from looking at stool. One of the telltale signs of whipworms is a stool that is covered with mucous at the tip, and the main symptom is weight loss.

External Parasites

Fleas are the most commonly found parasites in all mammals, including canines. Some dogs become so miserable from flea bites that they can scratch themselves raw, trying to ease the irritation. If your TT is scratching more than usual, check for fleas, and if you see any, get rid of them as quickly as you can. Most flea treatments are extremely effective and will solve the problem quickly if you don't let it get out of hand. Fleas often bite humans, too, usually going for legs and ankles and leaving small itchy bumps behind them.

The most common places you'll find fleas are at the base of your TT's ears and his rump. Look closely at areas where he has less hair, like his groin, to see if there are any signs of fleas there. Fleas can be more accurately diagnosed by parting your TT's hair in different places, looking for dark specs resembling poppy seeds. These are flea feces and are comprised of digested blood. If you're not sure, put it on a damp tissue, and after a short while, you'll see a red spot or halo develop as the blood rehydrates.

Ticks can potentially cause a few serious illnesses, including Lyme disease and Rocky Mountain Spotted Fever. There are more than 800 types of ticks globally, and they all feed on blood from mammals, birds, and reptiles. Given the health problems ticks can cause, it's important to get your TT screened annually for tick disease, as it's a mandatory requirement. Tick-borne diseases can be treated with broad-spectrum antibiotics.

Rather than check your TT daily to see if he has ticks, invest in a good tick collar, which will ensure he's tick-free for around eight months of the year when they are most active. If you have to remove a tick from your TT, use rubbing alcohol first and then pull the parasite out of his skin with tweezers. You want to make sure that you get the parasite's legs out from under the skin, where they hook in to get to your TT's blood supply. Infestations can be prevented by treating your TT with a tick-specific medication, dip, spray, or powder, which you can get from your vet.

Lice and mites are teeny tiny organisms that feed on your TT's skin, causing him to become itchy and potentially lose his hair. Generally speaking, mites and lice are different things, although they function in the same way. Lice live in a dog's hair and can be treated with the same medications as used for fleas and ticks. It's worth noting that the lice that live on dogs are not the same as the ones found on humans. Mites can cause mange and hair loss in different places around the dog's body, although generally, the forehead, eyes, muzzle, and forepaws. Mites can also cause scabies, which also affect humans when they burrow into the dog's skin. You'll see the signs if your TT shakes his head or scratches at his ears, and he'll have irritation on his legs, face, and elbows too.

Treatments for External Parasites

You'll find a wide range of products for the treatment of ticks, fleas, and other external parasites, including collars, solutions, shots, and pills available online. However, some products can cause your TT irritation or contain ingredients that are carcinogenic for both of you.

It doesn't help that some of these products, particularly tick collars, are extremely expensive, and if you have more than one dog, it can become prohibitive for some owners. As with most things relating to your TT's health, it's a good idea to consult with your vet to get a professional recommendation on the products most likely to get rid of external parasites without causing any additional problems.

CHAPTER 16
Caring for an Older Tibetan Terrier

The Basic Needs of an Older Tibetan Terrier

Tibetan Terriers have a life expectancy of between twelve and fifteen years. As he progresses closer to the age of 10, you'll start to notice signs that he's getting older. He'll be more prone to sleeping and less inclined to exercise than before, which is something that will become more noticeable as he ages.

Photo Courtesy of Susie Philip

Among the things you need to know as your TT gets older is that he will typically be much more sensitive to extreme temperature changes due to his metabolism slowing down with age. A senior TT is the same as an older person in that he will be less able to thermoregulate, so he won't be able to spend as much time outside in cold weather or when it's too hot.

Although your TT has been blessed with an extra protective double coat, many owners prefer to keep their dogs clipped short. If this is the case for your TT, you might want to consider getting him a blanket-like coat for outside wear, or you can let his coat return to its former glory for extra warmth.

Keeping your TT cool during hot weather is equally important, particularly if he isn't clipped short. However, as with humans, it's not as easy to remain cool as it is to keep warm. With cold weather, we can shelter inside or wear extra layers, but when it's hot outside, it's much harder to acclimatize comfortably. It's the same for your TT, especially if he's getting on in years.

Here are some ways you can help your TT beat the heat.

Hydration

The most important thing about hot weather is ensuring that your TT is always fully hydrated. He should always have access to fresh, cool water, and if his bowl has been sitting out for a while, check the temperature first and refill with cold water if it's a little warm. You can always throw a couple of ice cubes in the bowl if it's especially hot outside.

 Try adding around one-fourth of a cup of water to your TT's kibble to give him extra moisture in his food. This will make tasty gravy that he'll really enjoy too.

Turn up the AC

Although your TT may have been fine staying outside when he was younger, in his golden years, he should always have access to an air-conditioned space. Even if you have to go out, make sure the house will be as cool for your TT as if you were there yourself (albeit if you were wearing a fur coat).

If you don't have air conditioning, you can set up a fan in front of a bowl of ice or lay down a towel soaked in iced water to keep your TT cool. You can also place some frozen gel packs inside the covers of his bed.

Try Using Cool Foods

You can add foods like cucumber or apple to your TT's food, which will not only give him more moisture but will also help to reduce his body temperature. As a bonus, these tasty treats have great nutritional value, and they'll not only help to keep your TT cool but will also help him keep the pounds from piling on as his metabolism slows down.

 Coconut oil can really cool down your TT's food and will also give his skin and coat an extra healthy boost.

Walk Smart

It's just as important to keep your older TT active as it was in his younger years. Regular exercise will help him retain muscle mass and a good range of motion in his joints. However, walking your older TT needs a little fore-thought. Check the temperature outside and make sure it's not too hot or cold. If you're in the routine of taking your dog for a walk first thing in the morning, consider walking later in the day if it's very cold. Conversely, if you walk your dog when you return from work and it's hot outside, wait until sundown when your TT can enjoy his exercise much more.

 In the height of summer, set your alarm a little earlier so that you can take your TT out for a cool stroll before the sun starts blazing.

Know the Risk Factors

As mentioned above, older TTs have less ability to thermoregulate than when they were younger. There are several factors that can increase the risk of your TT suffering from heatstroke, such as:

- He's overweight.

- His coat is dark, which absorbs heat more readily.

- He has breathing problems and has difficulty panting to cool himself down.

 Make sure you take steps to keep your TT cool when temperatures start to rise and be vigilant of the following signs of overheating:
   - *Heavy panting and/or drooling*
   - *Rapid heartbeat*
   - *Dark or very red gums and tongue*
   - *Problem breathing*
   - *Dizziness, weakness, and agitation*

If any of these symptoms don't subside, take your TT to the vet immediately.

The Importance of Good Nutrition for a Senior Tibetan Terrier

> "
>
> *Tibetan Terriers age gracefully. They still enjoy the same things just not as often. Keep them on their good quality food, let them exercise at their own pace, and enjoy every day with them.*
>
> TANE KLEIST
> *Kildare Tibetan Terriers*
>
> "

Getting the right nutritional balance from his diet will ensure your TT has the best quality of life as he ages. As with developing puppies, the rate of change in senior dogs is equally fast-paced, which means they can deteriorate quickly if they become unwell. Whereas puppies need plenty of fuel to help them grow, a mature TT will not need as many calories, but he'll need a nutrient-rich diet.

Here are the most important nutritional elements of your senior TT's diet:

Water: Making sure your TT is always well-hydrated is possibly your biggest nutritional concern. If he doesn't drink enough and becomes dehydrated, he can become very sick, and mild dehydration can trigger pre-existing health conditions.

Protein: Your TT's requirement for protein remains the same throughout his adult life. Make sure his food has a high degree of digestible protein, preferably from a single source, and that will help him maintain healthy muscle mass.

Fat: Because your TT's metabolism will have slowed with age, he'll have a tendency to gain weight in the form of fat. For that reason, you should reduce the fat content of his food.

Minerals: Potassium and sodium are vital in maintaining the health of your TT's heart and kidneys, although over-supplementation can be damaging. He'll also benefit from calcium and phosphorous, but it's really important that these two minerals are given to him in the correct ratios for his health, so make sure you talk to your vet.

Carbohydrates: Strictly speaking, dogs don't require carbohydrates, as they generally get their energy from protein and fat sources. However, your older TT can benefit from complex carbohydrates, which are more nutrient-dense, higher in fiber, and have a lower glycemic index than simple carbs (which helps keep blood sugar levels stable). The best source of complex carbs you can feed your TT include brown rice, oats, wheat, quinoa, barley, or organ meat to give him more energy.

Vitamins: If you are feeding your TT a well-balanced, commercially available diet that meets AAFCO guidelines, supplemental vitamins and minerals are not necessary. Vitamin supplements designed for older dogs have no scientifically proven value. If your TT needs supplements, they should be directed to the specific need he has rather than because of his age. Always talk to your vet before giving your dog any supplements.

Anti-Arthritics: Omega-3 fatty acids are recommended for arthritis and will help to ease joint pain as your TT gets older.

Probiotics: Probiotics are typically drinks that contain beneficial bacteria. Probiotics are particularly useful for older TTs in treating certain intestinal infections and can help treat diarrhea. It's worth bearing in mind that although there is limited scientific research on probiotics, they are very unlikely to cause your dog any harm. As always, talk to your vet about any questions.

Provide Your Senior Tibetan Terrier with Proper Exercise

As your TT gets older, his mobility is likely to decline. But that doesn't mean he doesn't require any exercise. In fact, an active lifestyle will help reduce the onset of certain ailments attributed to old age like arthritis and loss of muscle mass. Although he might not be getting the 'zoomies' as frequently as he used to, there are still plenty of ways you can safely engage your aging TT in physical activity.

Exercise will also help him keep his mind occupied and regulate his weight to keep his body strong as he ages. Whatever physical limitations your TT has, there's always something fun you can do to keep him in optimal health.

Walking a Senior Dog

Your TT loves going on walks, and his enthusiasm for taking a stroll with his human companions doesn't dampen with age. Walking gives your TT low-impact exercise that is effective in promoting a healthy body and mind.

When your dog is a little older, you'll have to pay attention to your pace, the weather conditions, and how your TT feels during and after the walk.

You should also bear in mind that the surface you're walking on will impact your older TT's walking ability. Sand and grass are recommended surfaces as they are soft and easier to walk on than asphalt and gravel.

If your TT is showing signs of stiffness after his walk, you might want to shorten your outings to make things easier for him. The most important thing is to get out and enjoy the day, giving your TT a chance to experience new sights, smells, and sounds while out in the fresh air.

Exercising Your Senior Dog's Brain

Your senior TT will face many of the same challenges as older humans, including cognitive decline. As his body ages, his brain slows down, shrinking the older he becomes. However, it's not all bad news because research has shown there are ways to slow the aging process of a dog's brain by stimulating it with mental exercise.

Improved technology has allowed scientists to take MRI scans of a dog's brain, which has revealed how similar they are to our own brains. Cortical atrophy, also known as brain shrinkage, is something that both humans and canines go through as they age. However, it is also believed that the brains of both are particularly vulnerable to the free radicals the body's metabolism produces, causing damage.

The production of free radicals in an aging TT can cause brain dysfunction and, ultimately, brain death. To counteract this problem of free radicals, you can increase your TT's intake of antioxidants like Vitamin E and C, which are highly effective in protecting his brain.

Photo Courtesy of Michelle Watson

As mentioned above, keeping your TT active not only benefits his physical health, but it stimulates his mind too. Scientists have proven that exposing a dog of any age to new experiences, smells, sounds, and sights can help him maintain a healthy brain.

It will help if you mix up your senior TT's walk routine so that he's regularly experiencing different environments. He's a particularly curious creature and loves to explore, and that doesn't diminish with age.

If you need some help getting him out of your immediate area, take advantage of a travel product like a Dogger stroller. In a similar way to a child's stroller, the Dogger will give your TT the option of taking it easy if he's tired of walking and you're far from home. He'll enjoy looking around him as much as if he's walking.

Another activity you can try that your senior TT will love is problem-solving. Puzzle games are a great way of exercising a TT's mind, whatever his age.

Fun games can include:

- Hide-and-seek, using your dog's favorite treat or toy.
- The classic game where you hide a tasty treat under a cup and then your dog figures out how to get to it; add more cups to confuse him.
- Puzzle toys of all types are available in pet stores and usually involve some type of reward system. You can make sure he's having healthy snacks like chunks or apple or carrot.

Managing Your Tibetan Terrier's Typically Age-Related Health Problems

Tibetans are good at hiding medical issues. If you notice behaviors that are not normal for your dog, discuss with your vet. They may no longer want to accompany you on long walks or run and play as much. Give them the freedom to do what is comfortable for them. Most often they just want a warm soft bed to rest in and their person to cuddle up with.

RENE' STAMM
Euphoria Tibetans

Here are some common age-related health issues your TT may experience as he gets older and what you can do to help him:

Deafness: It is common for older TTs to lose their hearing gradually due to nerve damage. Although nothing can be done to stop the deafness, much can be done to help him adapt. Many owners will at first mistake hearing loss for dementia, as your TT may display a similar type of confusion. Fortunately, deafness in dogs is fairly easy to handle, and because he'll lose hearing gradually over time, you'll have time to adapt. Try specific methods for deaf dog training, like the use of hand signals. Soon, you will find that the hearing loss hardly affects your TT's day-to-day life.

Blindness: Like deafness, many older TTs experience a gradual loss of vision. This is usually due to degenerative changes in the eye but can be caused by an eye disease like cataracts, which Tibetan Terriers are prone to. If the blindness is simply due to old age, nothing can be done to reverse it. Fortunately, dogs have other senses that help them adjust to the loss of their eyesight. Just be sure to take it slow with your TT and keep him on a leash at all times if outdoors. Your TT will be familiar with the layout of your home, which will make it easier for him to adapt. Try and refrain from rearranging your furniture, too, often as it will confuse him.

Dementia/Cognitive Dysfunction: TTs can exhibit developmental changes as they age that are similar to dementia and Alzheimer's Disease in humans. Although the signs are subtle at first, they can become very severe and result in poor quality of life. The symptoms of dementia in TTs include disorientation, pacing/wandering, confusion, standing still as if lost, less interest in interacting with the family, etc. While there is no cure for dementia or cognitive dysfunction, there are medications and supplements that may help in some cases, and you should consult your vet.

Incontinence: Old age causes changes to the organs, muscles, and nerves in the body and can make it harder for your TT to "hold it" the way he used to. Incontinence can be a sign of many different diseases, so it is essential to have your vet rule some things out. If there is no other medical reason for incontinence, you'll need to adjust your schedule to let your dog out for "potty breaks" more often.

Kidney Disease: Aging takes a toll on the kidneys, so it is not uncommon for older TTs to develop kidney disease. Chronic kidney (renal) disease is usually a gradual process that begins as renal insufficiency and progresses to full renal failure. There is no cure for this disease, but there are, fortunately, many ways to treat it. Signs of kidney disease include increased thirst and urination, loss of appetite, nausea, and lethargy. Starting your TT on a prescription kidney diet can be very effective.

Holistic Therapies for Your Older Tibetan Terrier

Although many health problems your older TT may get don't have cures, there are some great holistic therapies available specifically for older dogs that can really help them.

Some of these therapies are the following:

ACUPUNCTURE

Acupuncture for dogs? Yes, it's a thing, and it can help a range of senior TT issues. As with human acupuncture, it involves strategically placed needles or a therapeutic laser that helps direct the flow of energy through the body. Acupuncture can help TTs suffering from inflammatory conditions, such as spinal problems, hip dysplasia, and other forms of arthritis. It can also help relieve gastrointestinal conditions, such as colitis and inflammatory bowel disease, and prevent chronic stomach problems, neurological problems, and postsurgical pain.

Photo Courtesy of Julie Thomas

HYDROTHERAPY

Hydrotherapy involves using water to help soothe and heal sore muscles and joints. It's similar to how humans use hot tubs or warm baths to relieve soreness, but it goes a step further. Warm water helps the muscles relax and ease joint pain to allow for your older TT to be more comfortable when he exercises. The water supports his weight, which helps with pain relief and increases the range of motion in stiff joints.

MASSAGE

Everyone loves a massage, and your older TT is no exception! Massage is a rehabilitation-type therapy used along with exercises and stretching to help alleviate pain. Massage is the practice of rubbing muscles to reduce pain, tension, and anxiety. Massage helps reduce pain and anxiety by improving cardiovascular and lymph system circulation in the dog's body. It also helps induce relaxation and give comfort to an older TT.

Knowing When it's Time to Say Goodbye

The unavoidable reality of keeping any pet is that he will eventually pass away either from old age, illness, or accident. As with grief over a human loss, there is no manual telling you how to cope with it. Everyone deals with the loss of their TT in different ways, which should always be respected.

Your TT may pass away peacefully on his own, but there is always the possibility of having to face the hardest choice of whether to euthanize him. Some people want their dogs to live so much that they allow them to live on despite having a poor quality of life. Although it's the toughest thing many of us have to do in life, we have to know when it's time to let our dogs go.

When it comes to your TT, there's never going to be a "best time to say goodbye to him. Nevertheless, you should know the main indications that will tell you that the time has come so that you can do the best you can to help him.

Terminal illness

An illness is classed as terminal if it can no longer be treated. In terms of expense, it costs less to euthanize a dog that has a terminal disease than

Photo Courtesy of Alice T. Boggs

it does to keep him alive with medication and treatment. In fact, keeping a terminally dog alive often only adds to his misery.

Pain

If your TT is in so much pain that medication is unable to help him, it's only fair to end his suffering. Signs of pain in your TT include:

- Excessive grunting and groaning
- Excessive panting
- Trembling
- Limping
- Restlessness and agitation
- Loss of appetite
- Excessive scratching or licking a particular body part

If your dog's quality of life falls beyond a reasonable standard and there's nothing more you can do, it's time to consider euthanasia.

Here are some signs that your TT is still enjoying a good quality of life:

- He has a good appetite and is eating well.
- He is drinking enough to be sufficiently hydrated.
- He is able to go to the bathroom without assistance.
- He responds enthusiastically to his favorite family members and toys.
- He still has decent mobility and gets excited when it's time for a walk.

Your TT should experience more good days than bad days in order for you to determine he has a sustainable quality of life.

Loss of vital bodily functions

If your TT is no longer able to perform basic bodily functions like urinating and defecating on his own, it's probably time to say goodbye. Dogs in this condition will remain in one position until they are moved and can develop sores from lying in their own mess.

Breathing difficulties

Breathing problems are very distressing for an older Tibetan Terrier, and once they have developed, it's very difficult to treat them. You have to ask yourself if you can endure watching this kind of suffering or if it's better to give your dog permanent rest.

What about Euthanasia?

If you have made the very difficult decision to euthanize your older TT, you will also need to decide how and where you and your family will say the final goodbye.

Euthanasia involves an injection that contains an overdose of an anesthetic drug which will allow your TT to gently drift into unconsciousness. The procedure is usually carried out on the vet's table, and you can choose who can be present. You should prepare yourself for the experience of seeing the life leave your beloved TT's body painlessly as he appears to fall asleep under the influence of the drugs.

After the point when your TT has passed away, there can sometimes be muscle twitches or intermittent breathing. Your TT may also release his bladder or bowels, which is normal.

Your vet will then use a stethoscope to check that your TT's heart is no longer beating.

Before the procedure is scheduled to take place, make sure that all members of your family have time with your TT to say a private goodbye.

If you have children, make sure that you explain the decision to them and prepare them for saying goodbye to him one last time ahead of the procedure. This may be your child's first experience with death, and it is very important for you to help her or him through the grieving process. Books that address the subject, such as When a Pet Dies by Fred Rogers or Remembering My Pet by Machama Liss-Levinson and Molly Phinney Baskette, may be very beneficial in helping your child to deal with this loss.

It is an individual decision whether or not you and your family want to be present during the euthanasia procedure. For some pet owners, the emotion may be too overwhelming, but for many, it is a comfort to be with their pet during the final moments. It may be inappropriate for young children to witness the procedure since they are not yet able to understand death and may also not understand that they need to remain still and quiet.

Some veterinarians will come to your house, which allows both the pet and the family to share their last moments together in the comfort of their own home.

Cremation vs. Burial

The choice of whether to opt for cremation or burial of your TT's remains is entirely your preference, and there is no right or wrong decision. More than 90% of pets of all types are cremated, with the remaining being buried, which is a much higher rate for cremation than for humans.

Many factors are taken into account when deciding between the two, including costs, available options, and the right space to bury your TT.

If you have chosen euthanasia for your TT, you will probably get his ashes handed to you within a week of his passing, as your vet will organize his cremation. Alternatively, if you go to a pet crematorium, you can often get his ashes back to you on the same day.

If you wish to bury your TT, you should do so as soon as possible after his death. Most pet cemetaries provide a pickup service to transport your TT's remains for burial. If you decide to bury your TT yourself or it's a weekend or holiday and the pet cemetary is closed, many vet offices will store your TT's remains for a few days until you're able to bury him.

Grieving the Loss of Your Tibetan Terrier

Grief over the loss of a beloved pet can be overwhelming and all-consuming. It's also a very delicate situation for any children in your family. Consider the following after your TT has departed as a way of helping everyone who loved him to grieve:

- Explain the loss to young children in a way that they'll understand. It's important that children appreciate that death comes to us all. Although it may be tempting to protect their feelings, you also don't want to confuse them. Be honest but really gentle with your children's feelings and tell them how much you are hurting too.

- Allow all family members to grieve. Losing a dog is a very traumatic time, but everyone has different ways of responding. Don't expect any family member to "snap out of it" or just "move on." Let everyone who loved your TT take their own time coming to terms with his departure.

- Don't hold back from expressing your emotions. There's no doubt that you will feel sad, and you might even feel despair, guilt, or anger. Rather than bottling things up and trying to be strong, give yourself permission to grieve as openly and for as long as you need to.

- Create a ceremony or service to honor your TT. In the same way as a funeral does for a human, a dedicated service allows everyone in the family a sense of closure. Give everyone a chance to say a few words, and even create a memorial for your TT in a special place at home.

- If you have other pets, be mindful that they will notice the loss of their TT chum too. Maintain their schedules so that they have the security of their usual routine, and keep an eye out for any signs of depression, such as loss of appetite or interest in normal activities.

- Reach out to friends and relatives for support. Don't assume that others will think you're silly for grieving the loss of your TT.

Ultimately, although your TT may no longer be with you, your life has been touched by one of the most sensitive and loving dogs around. Treasure your memories. Remember him with joy, and be happy in the knowledge that he is no longer in any pain.

When you lose a beloved dog, it can be very tempting to fill the painful gap he left behind by getting another one. As with all aspects of handling grief, there is no right or wrong way to go about it. That said, it's important that you understand your reasons for wanting another dog so that you make the right decision.

Everyone handles grief differently, and for some, bringing a new pet into their home while still grieving the loss of their TT isn't the best decision for either them or the new pet. On the other hand, a new pet could distract from grief and reduce the loneliness many feel when they lose a treasured TT. Ultimately, that decision is yours and only needs to be considered when the time is right.

Made in the USA
Las Vegas, NV
25 March 2022

46290999R00105